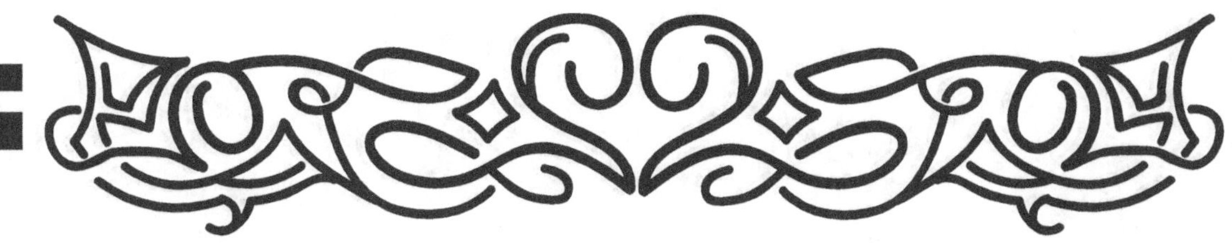

This Belongs To

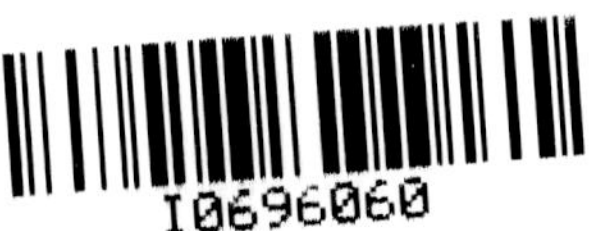

____

____

____

Butterfly Fish

Coloring Book

For Kids

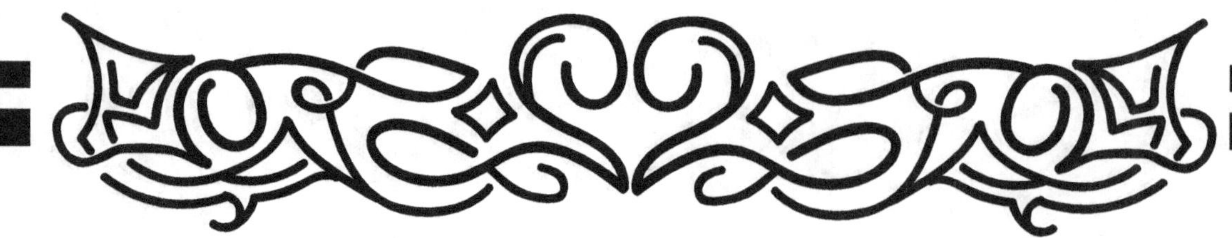

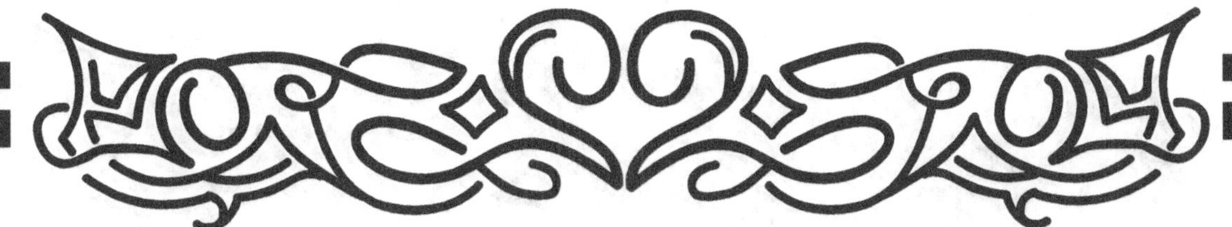

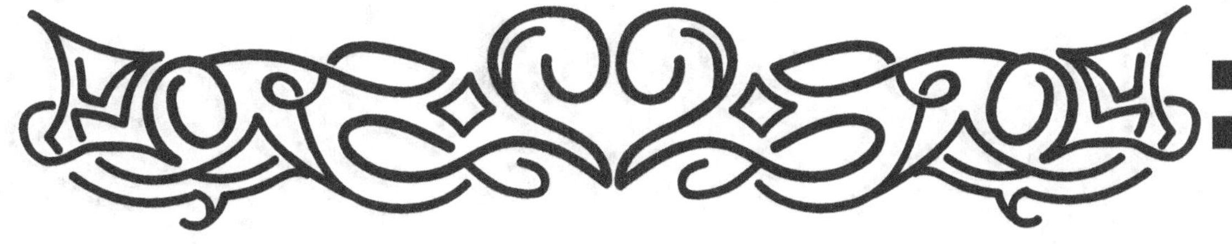

Test Your Color

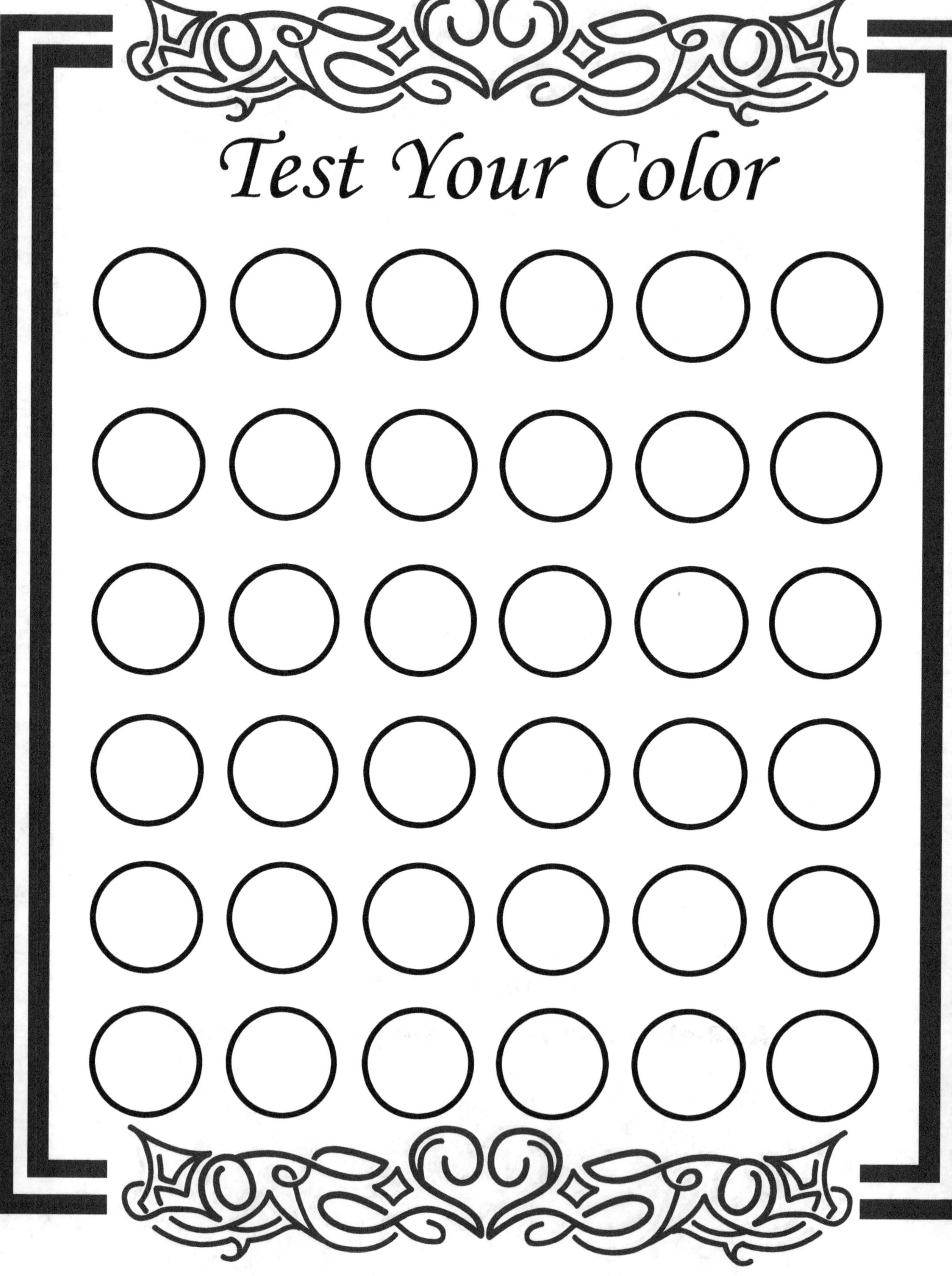

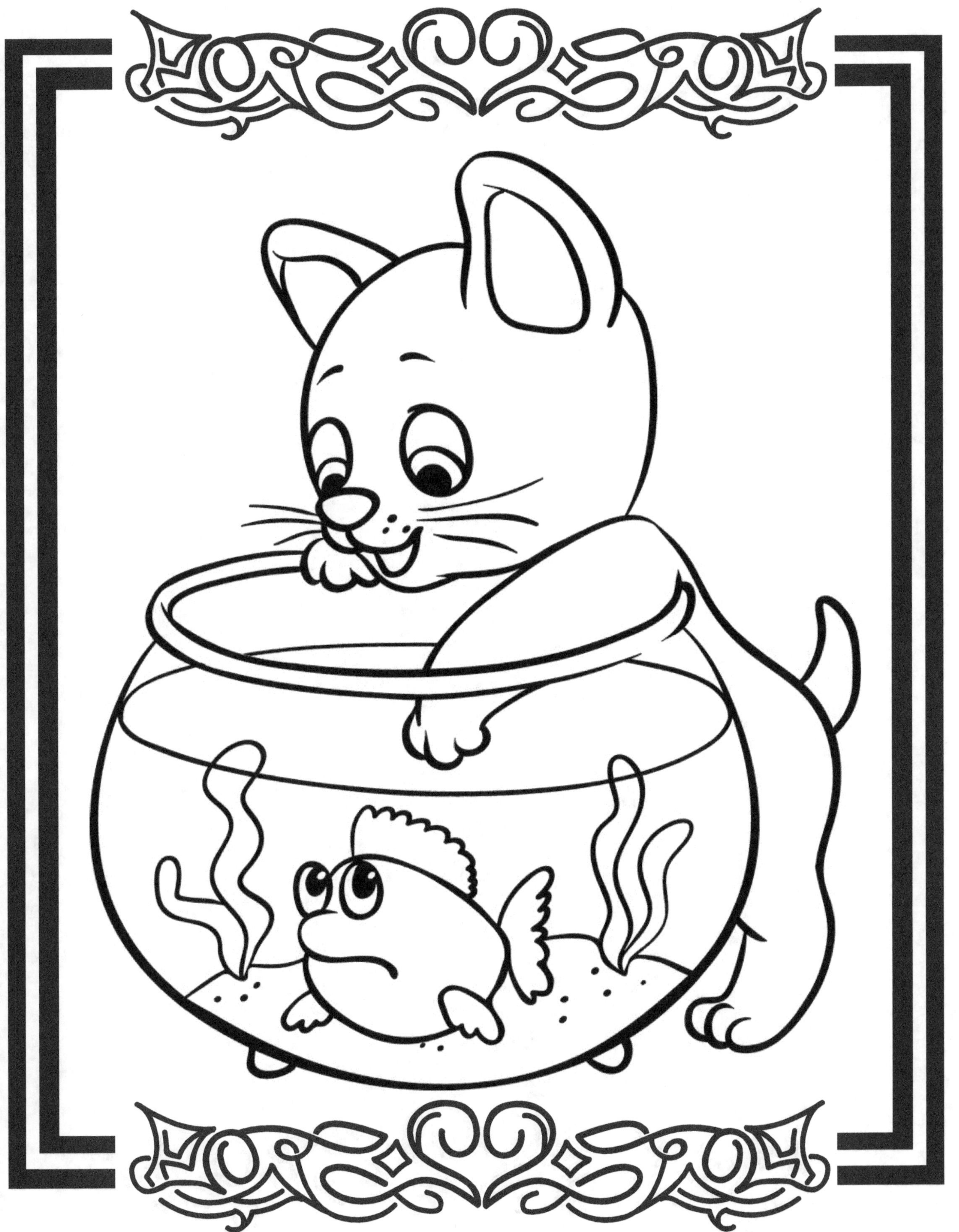

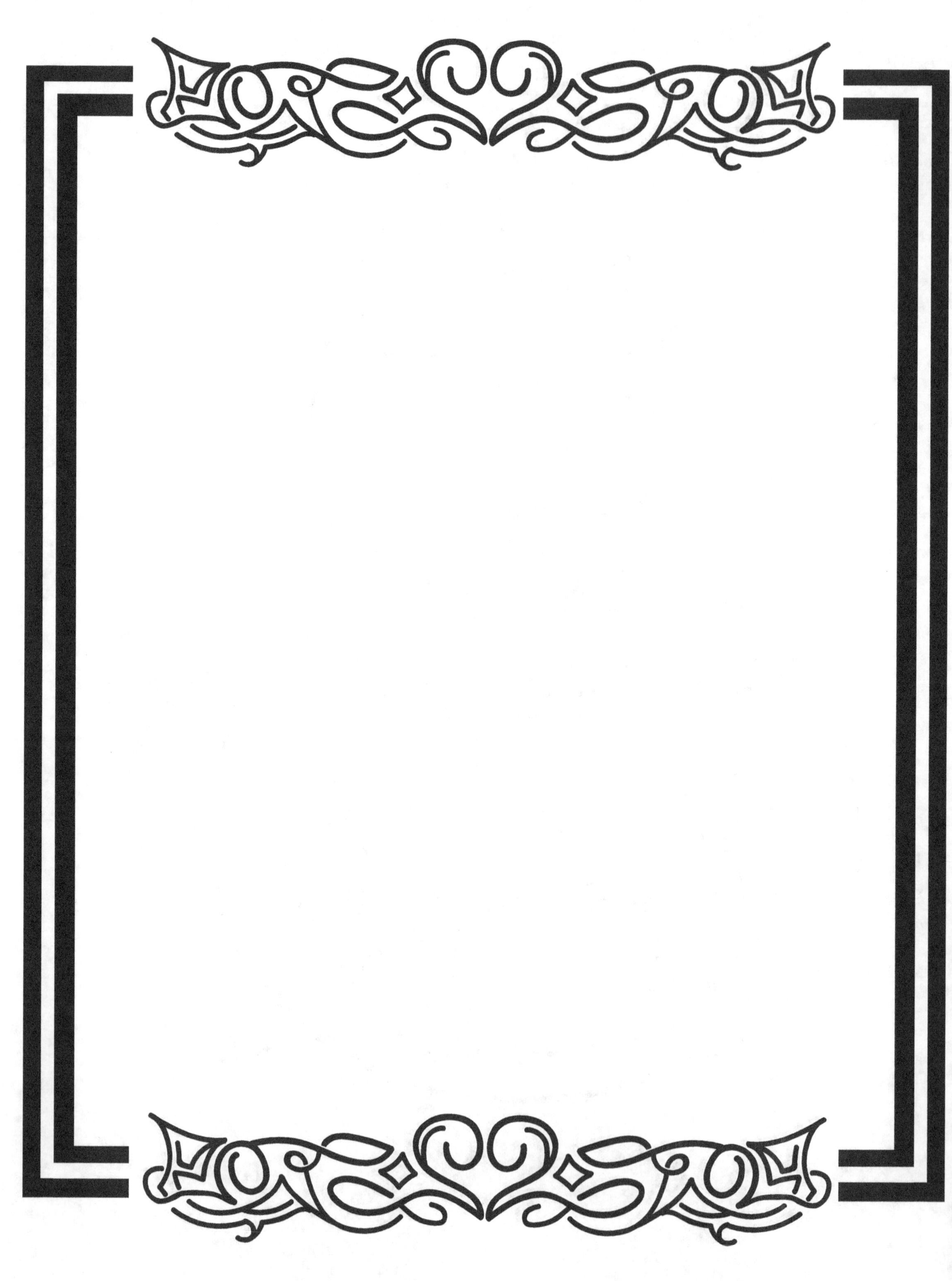

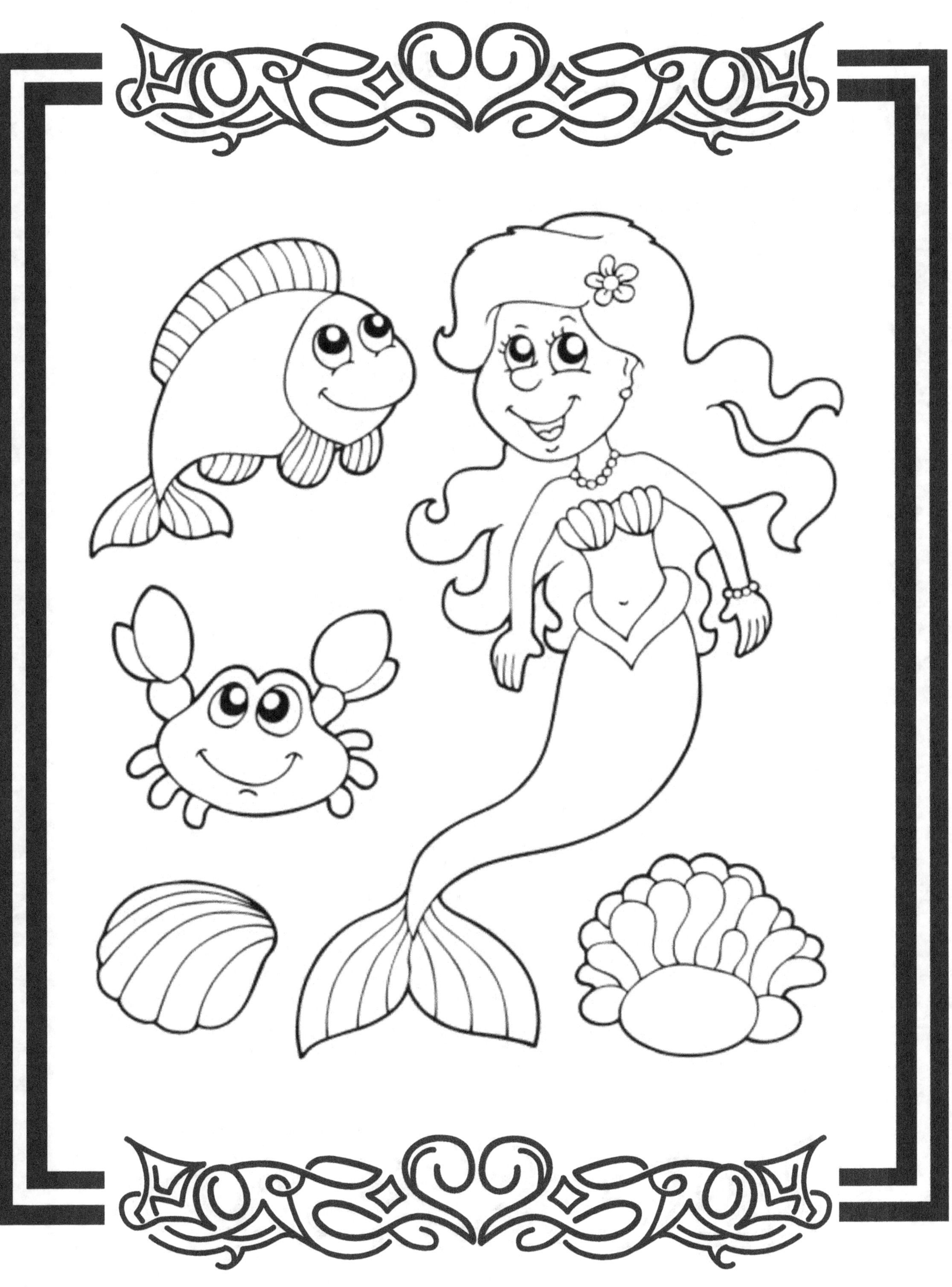

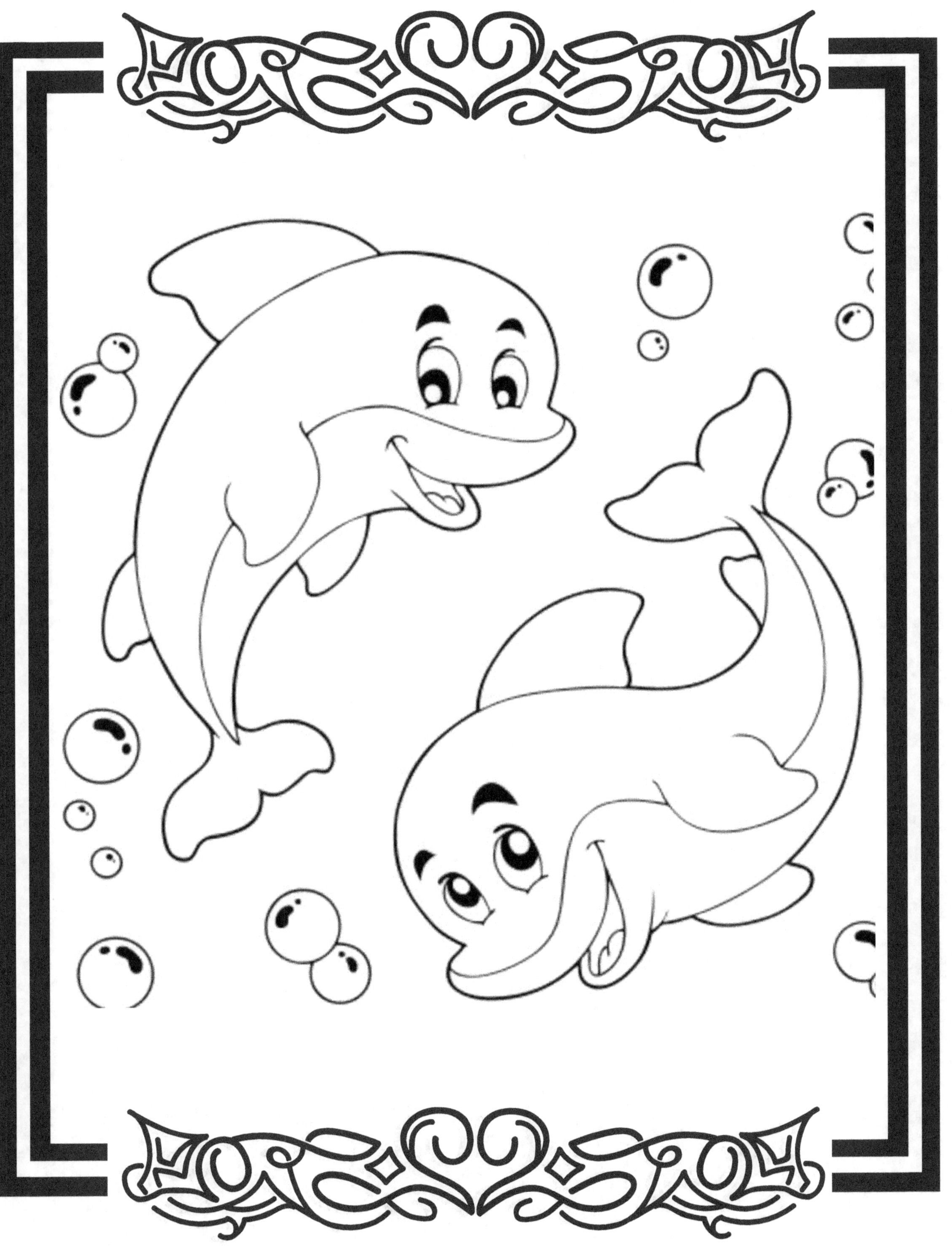

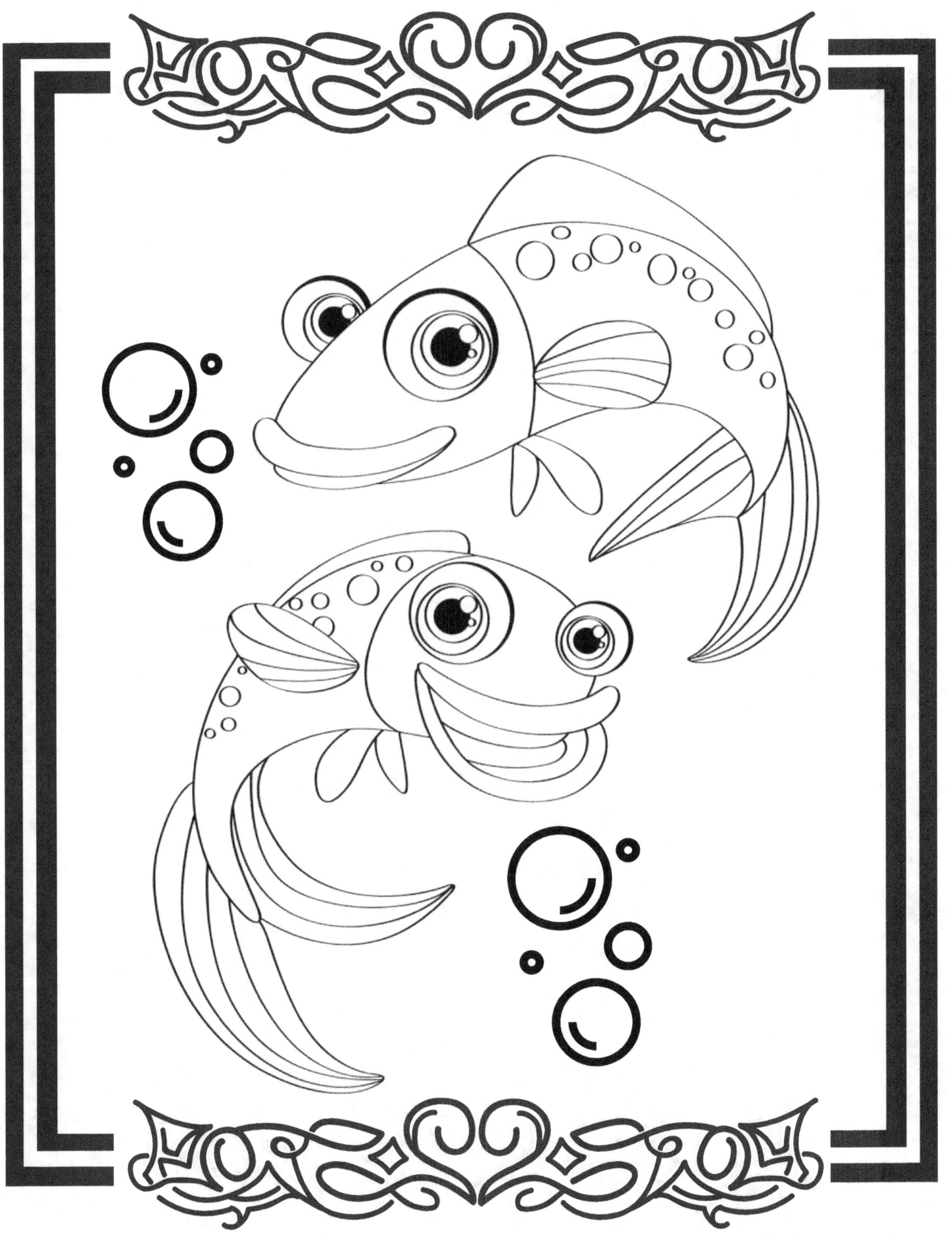

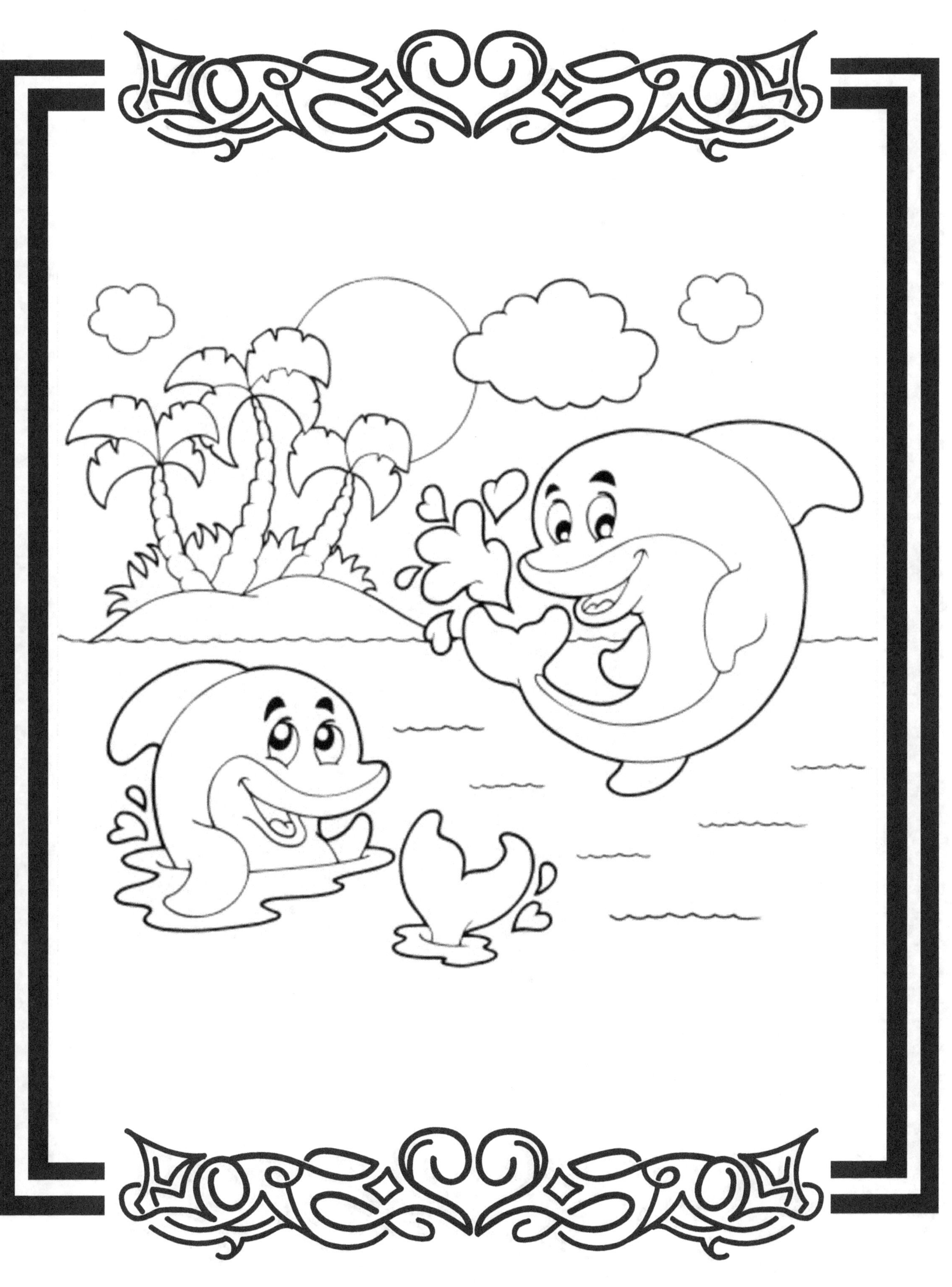

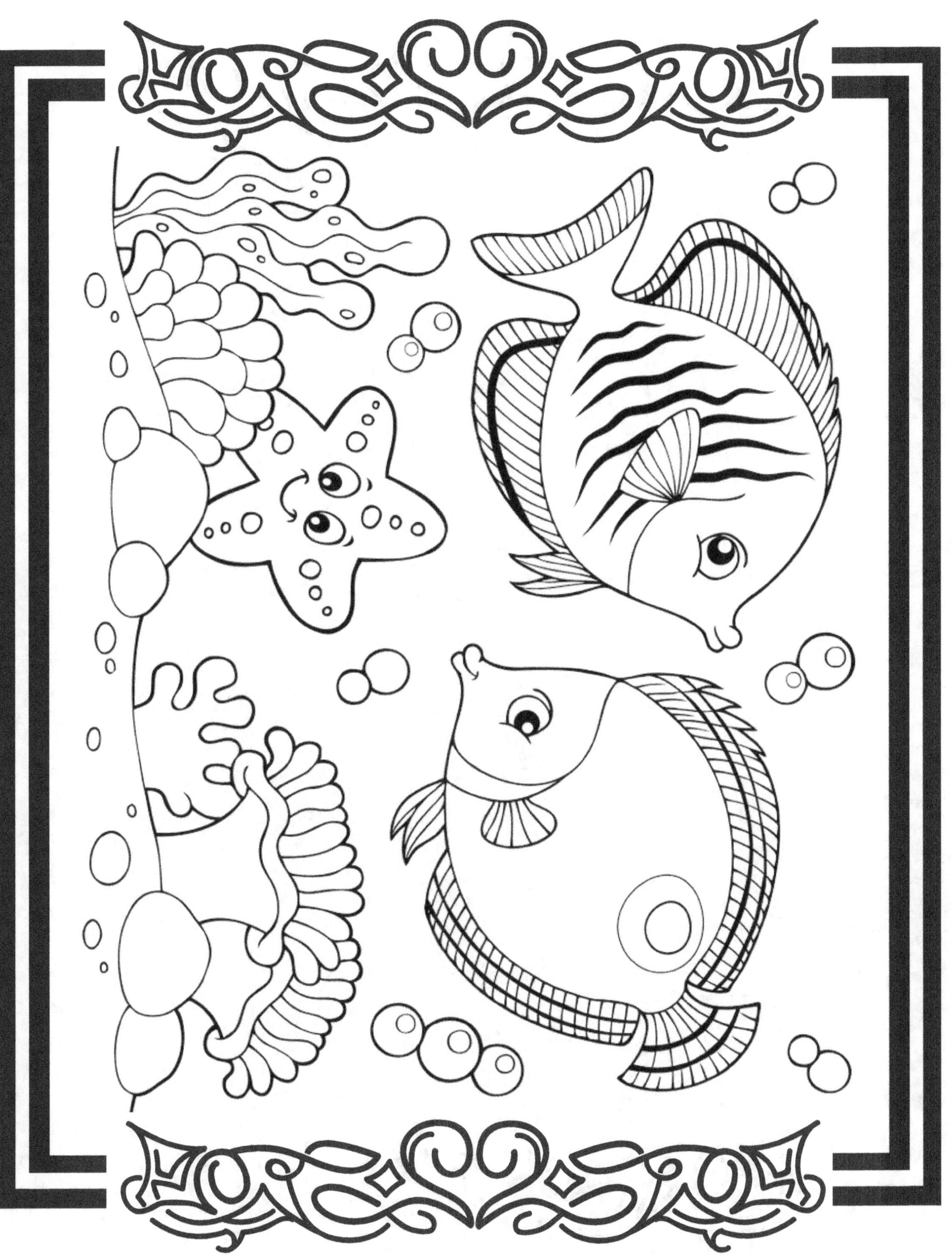

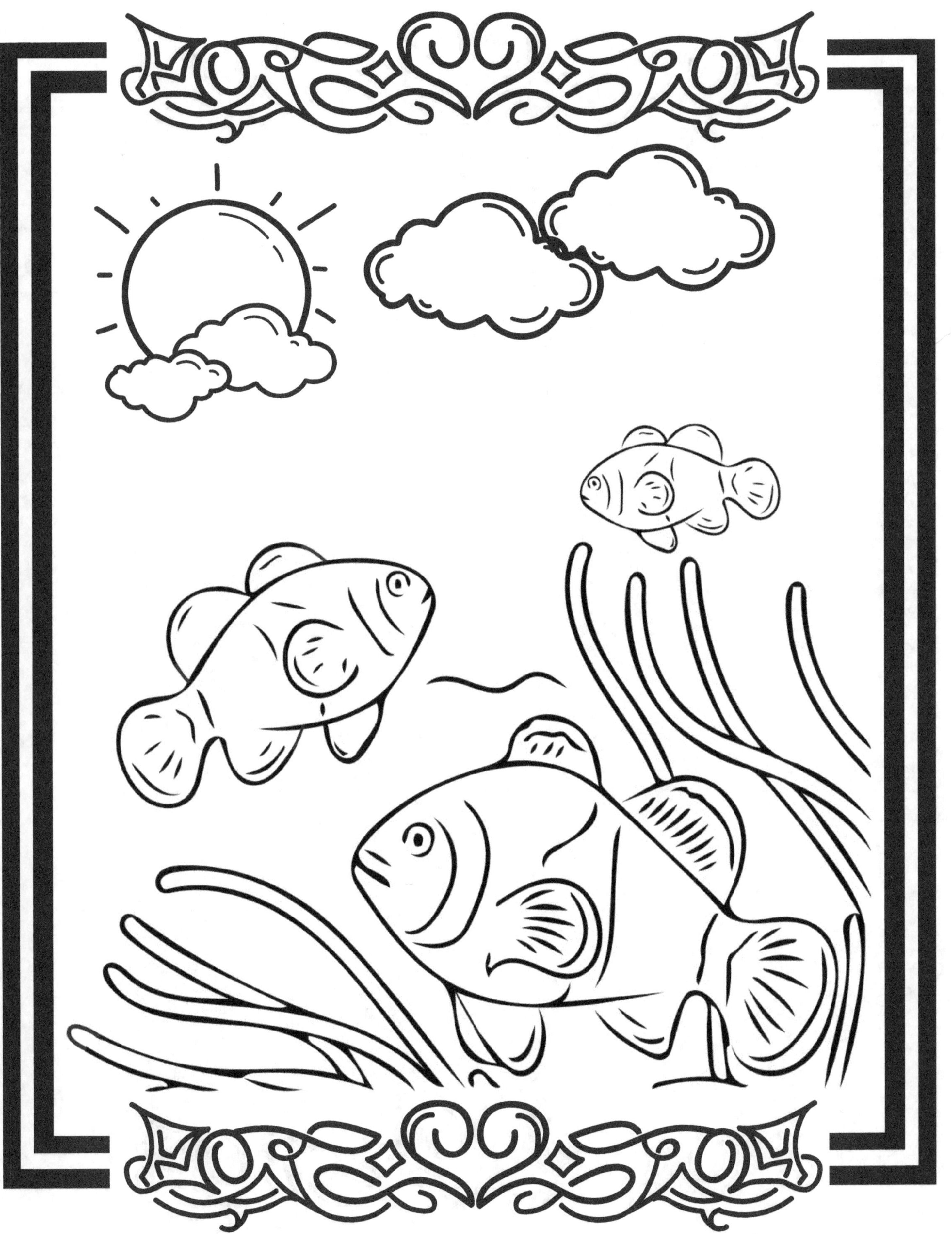

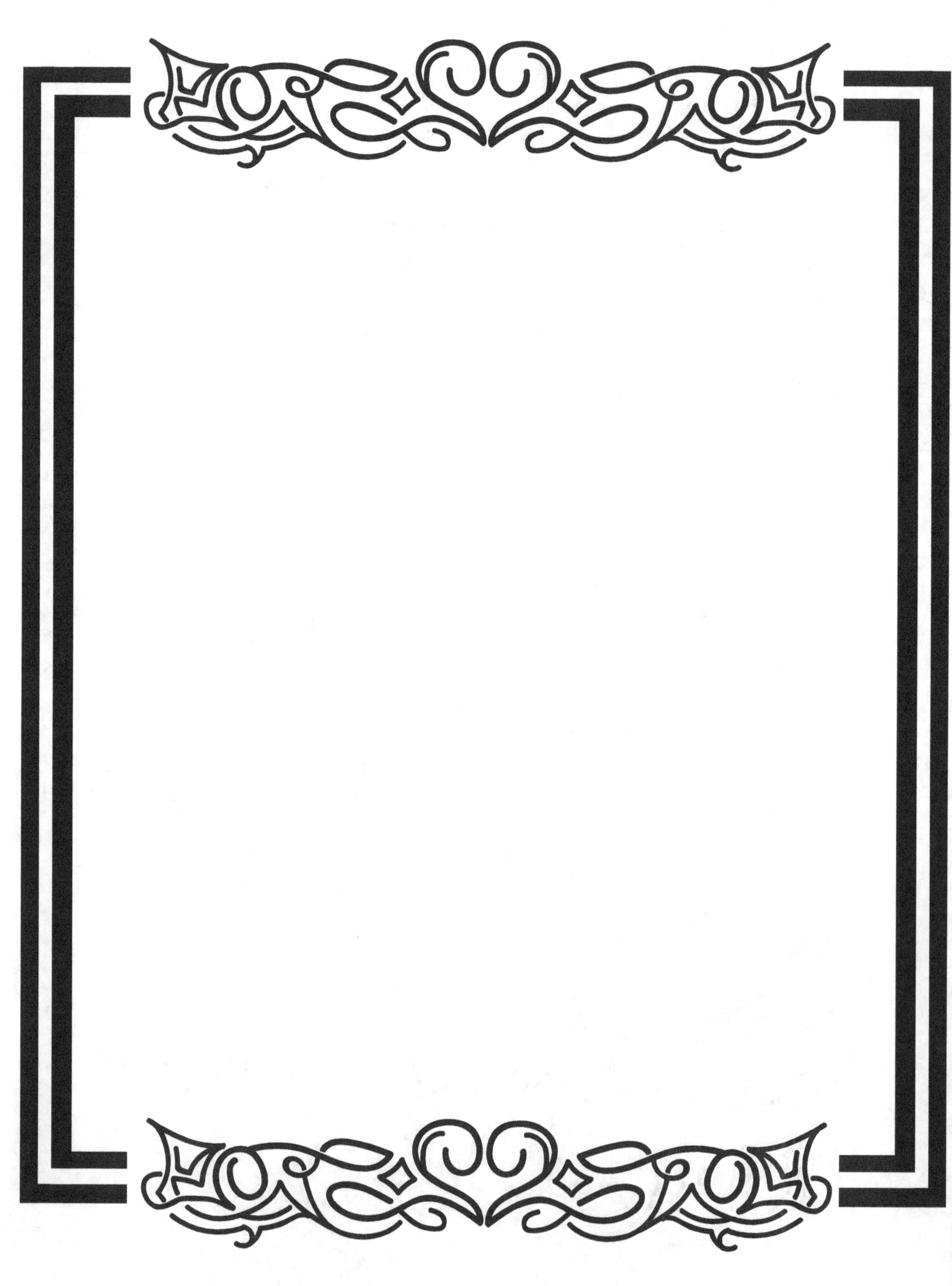

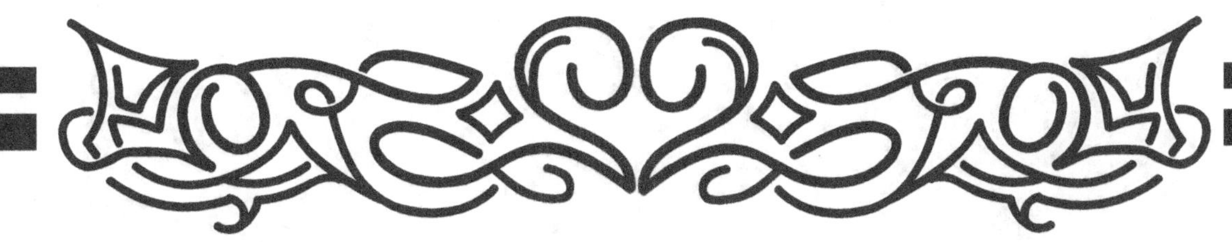

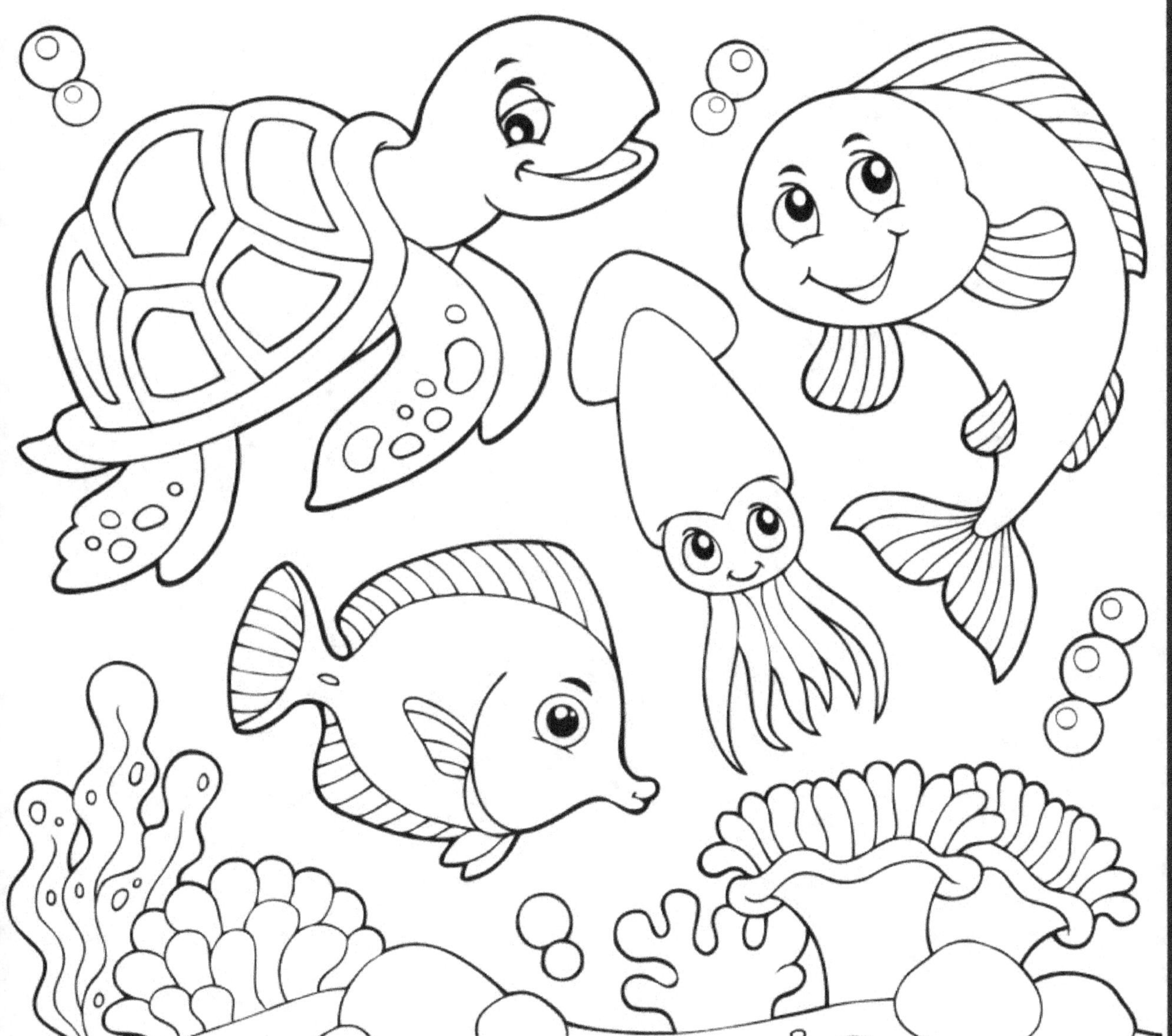

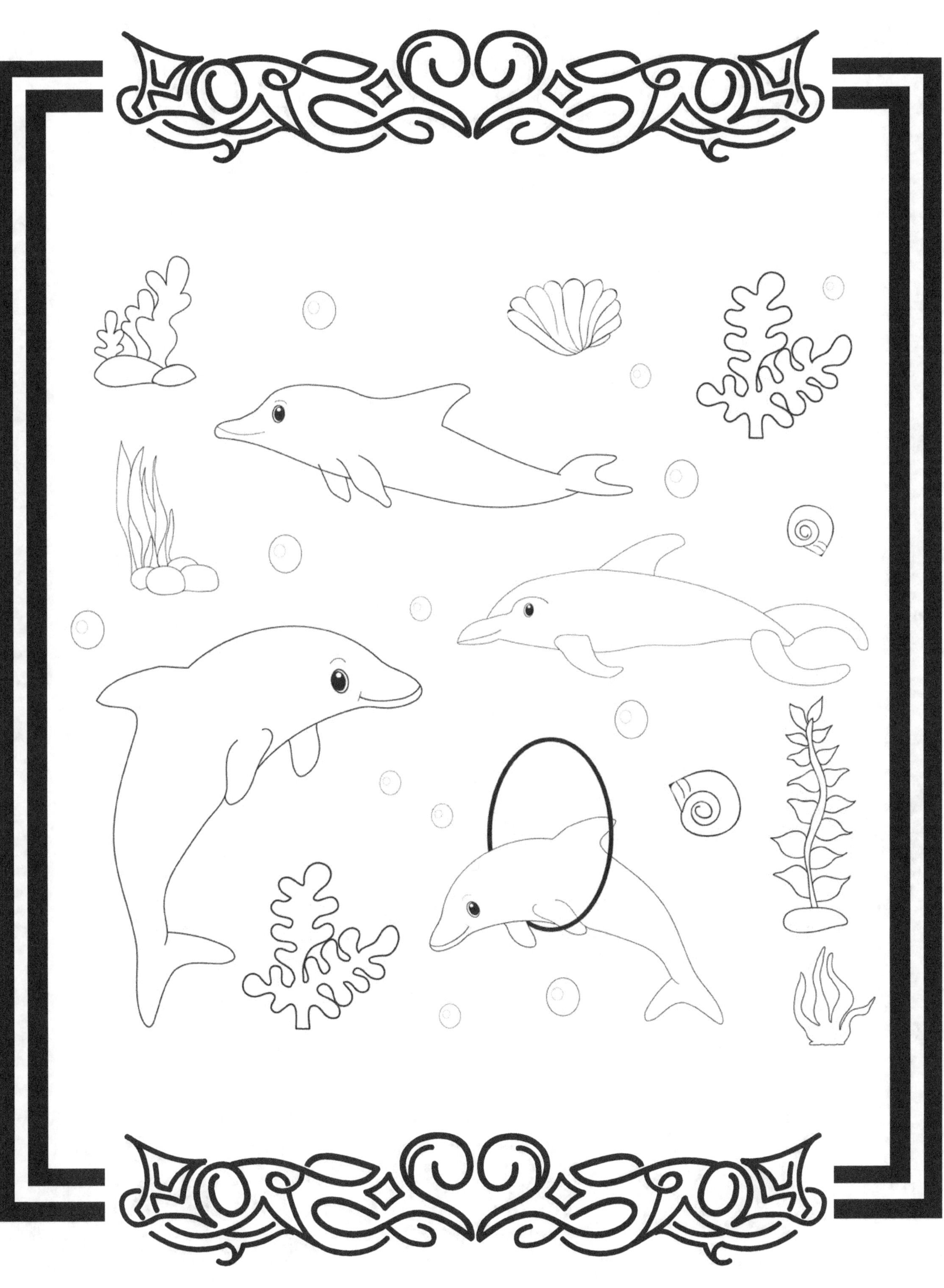

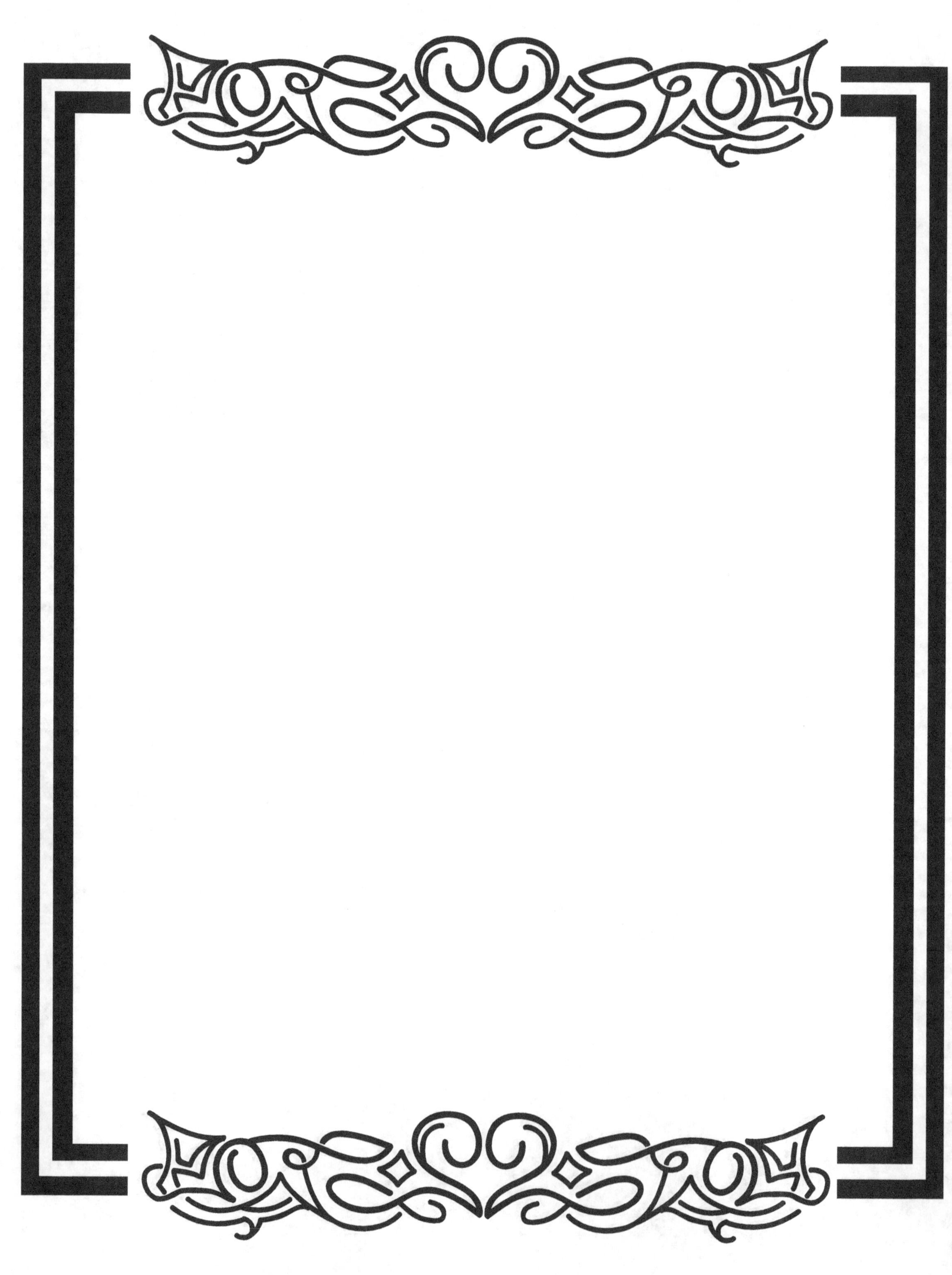

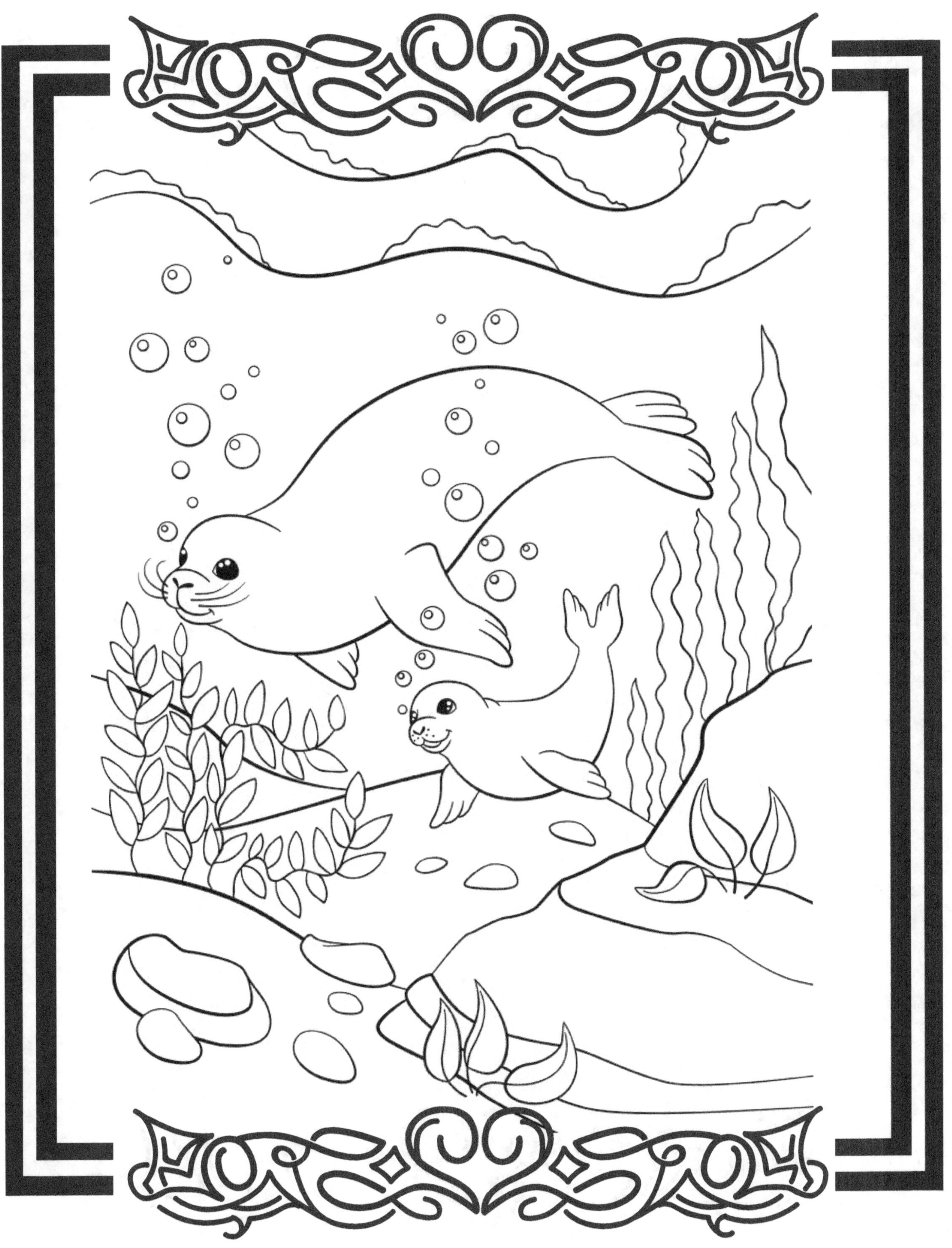

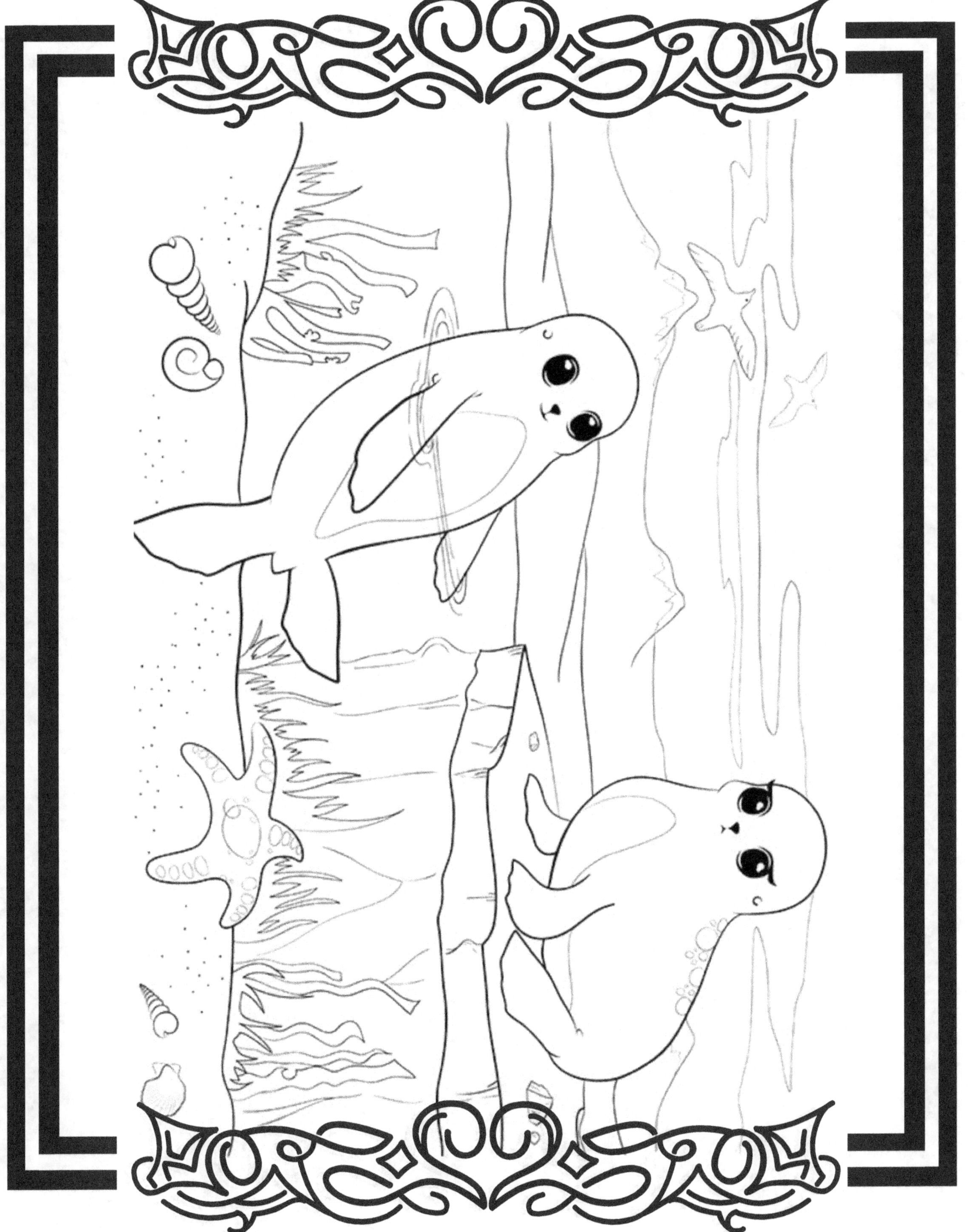

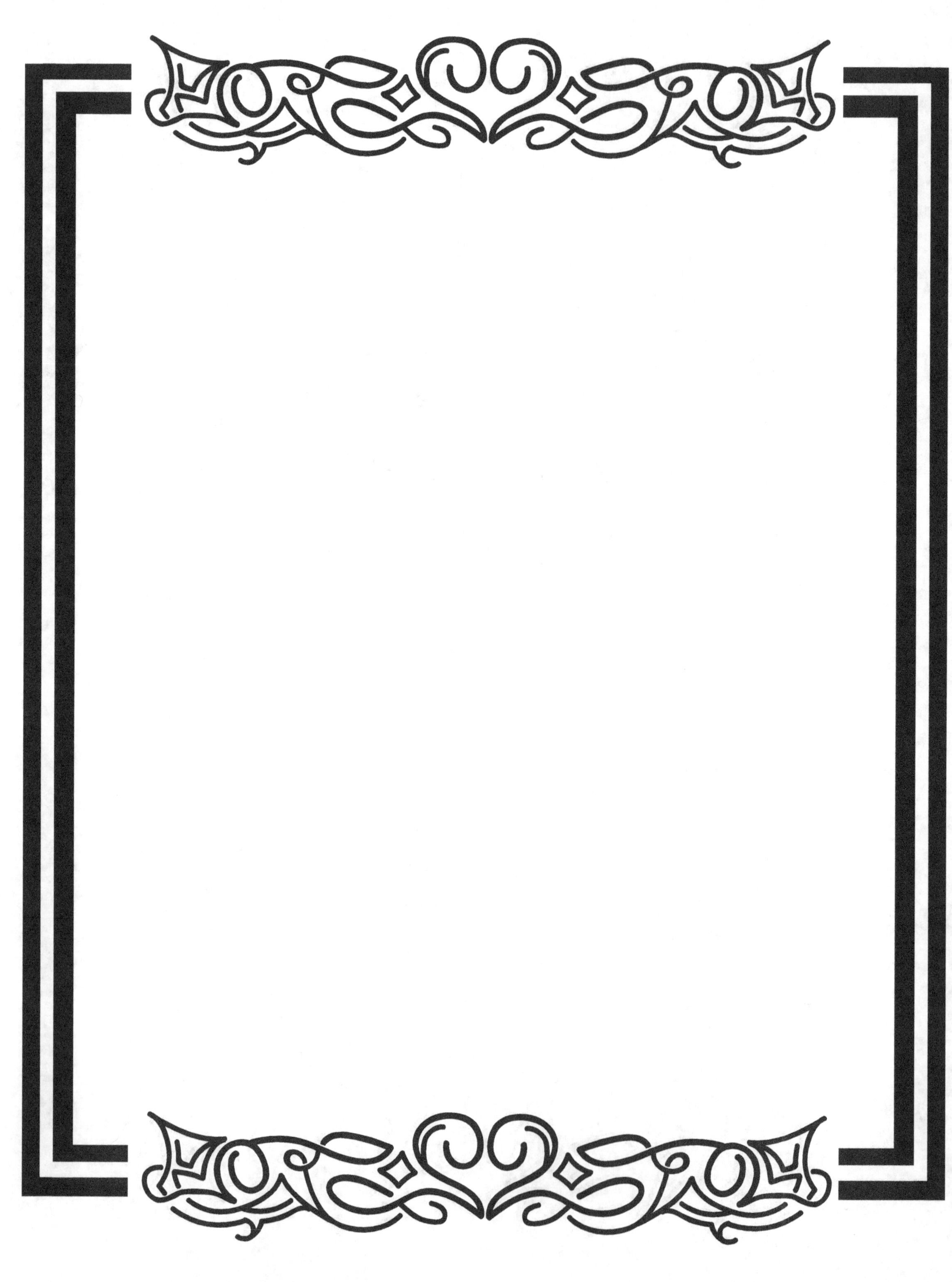

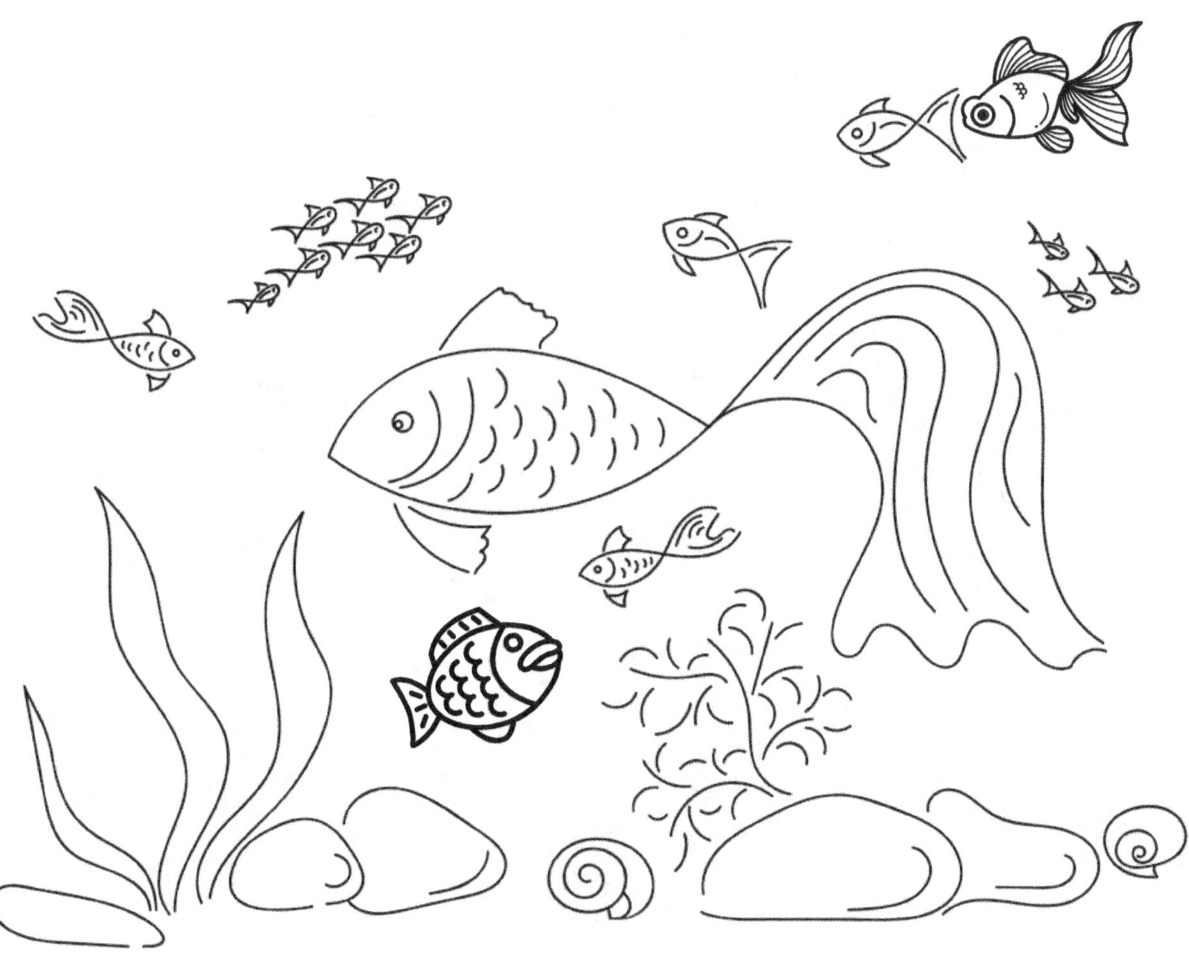

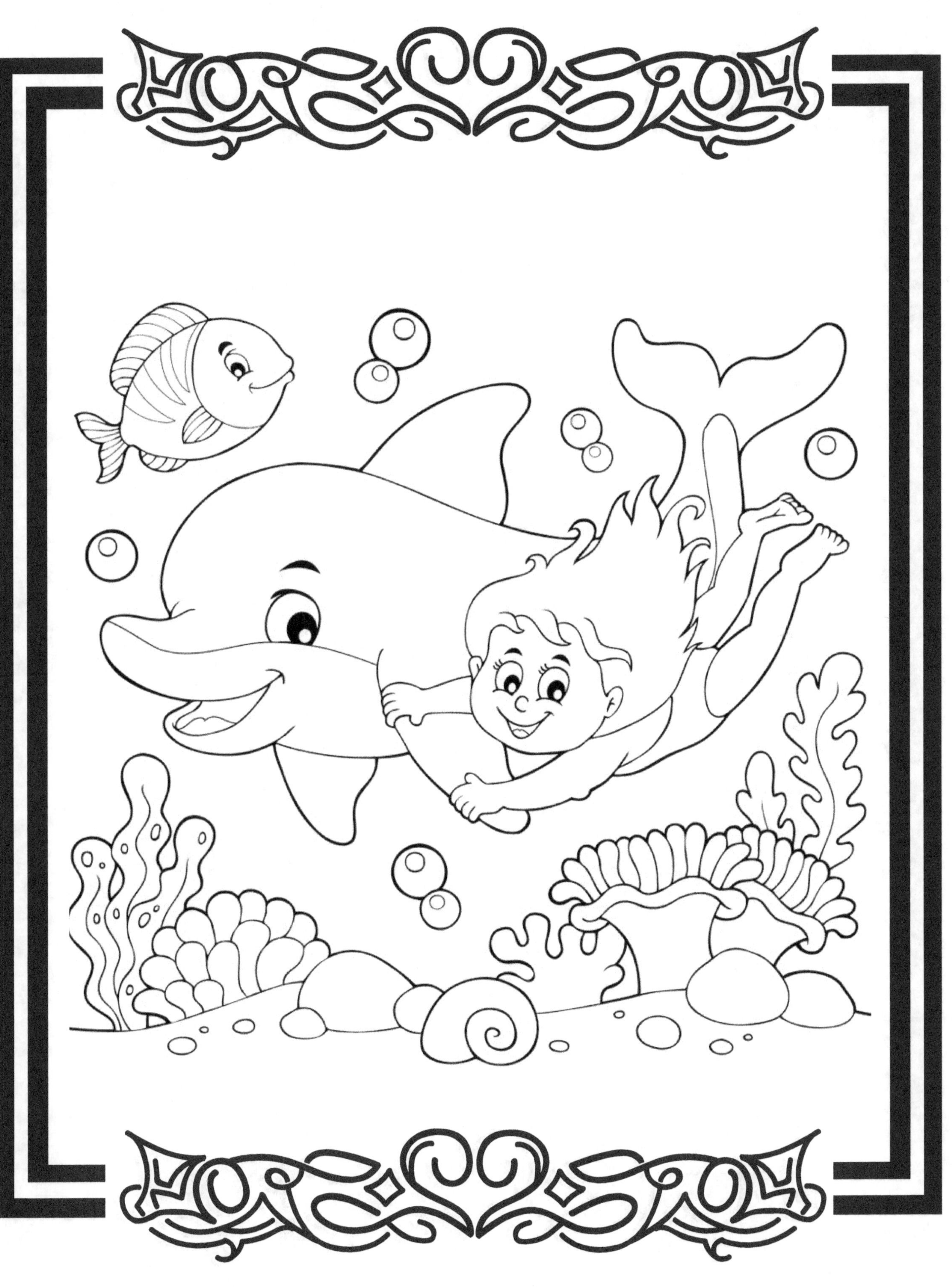

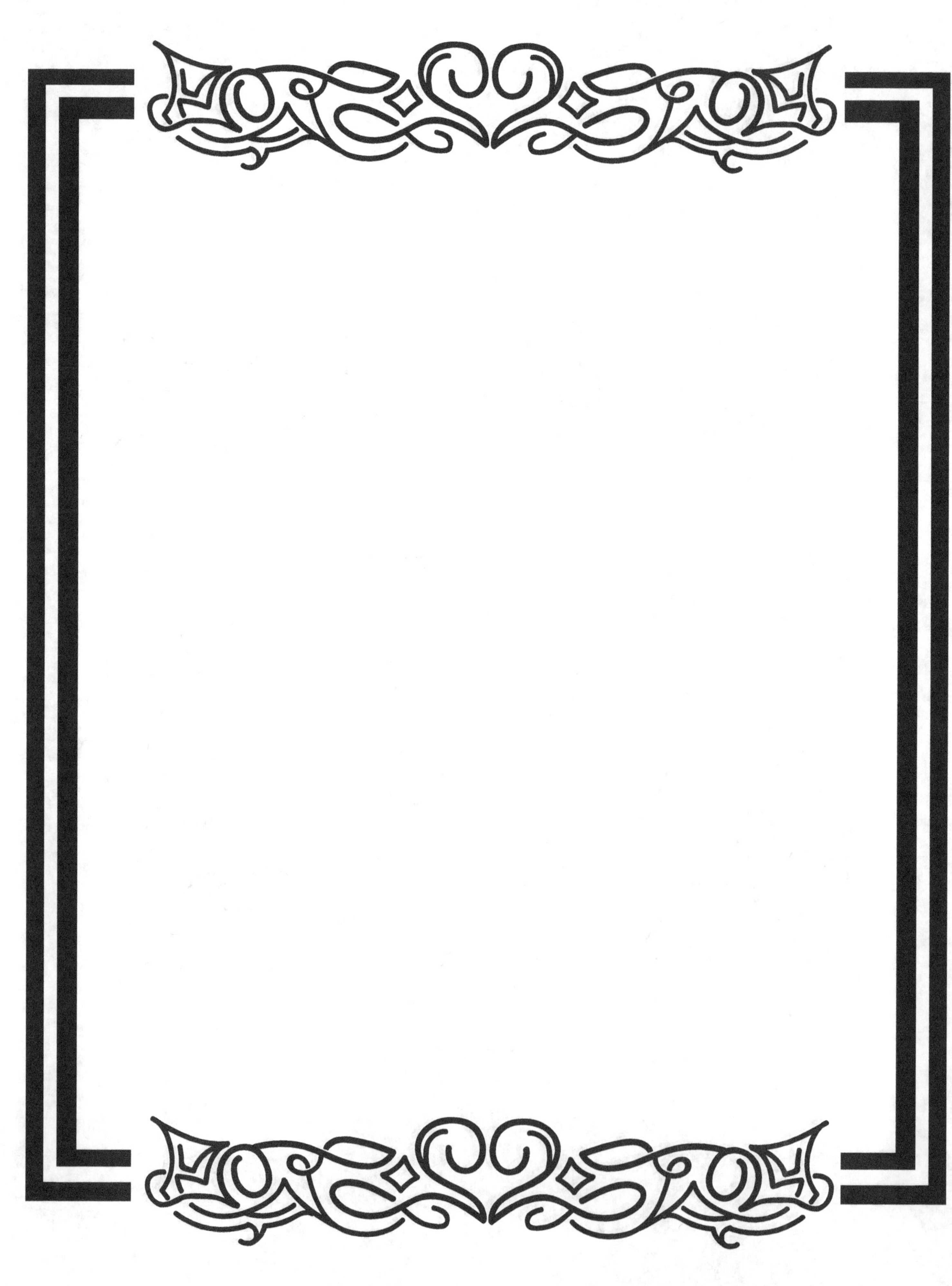

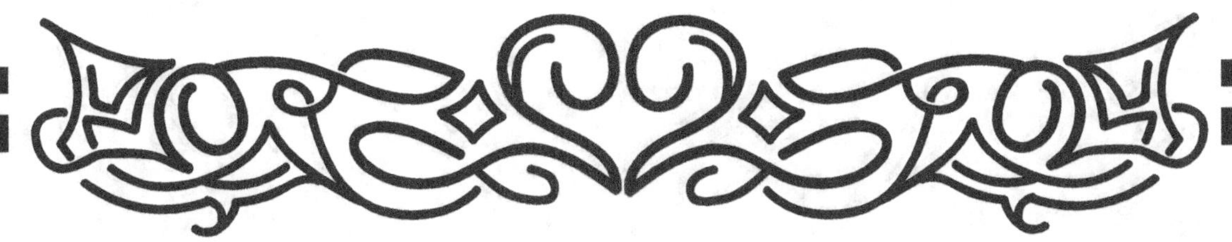

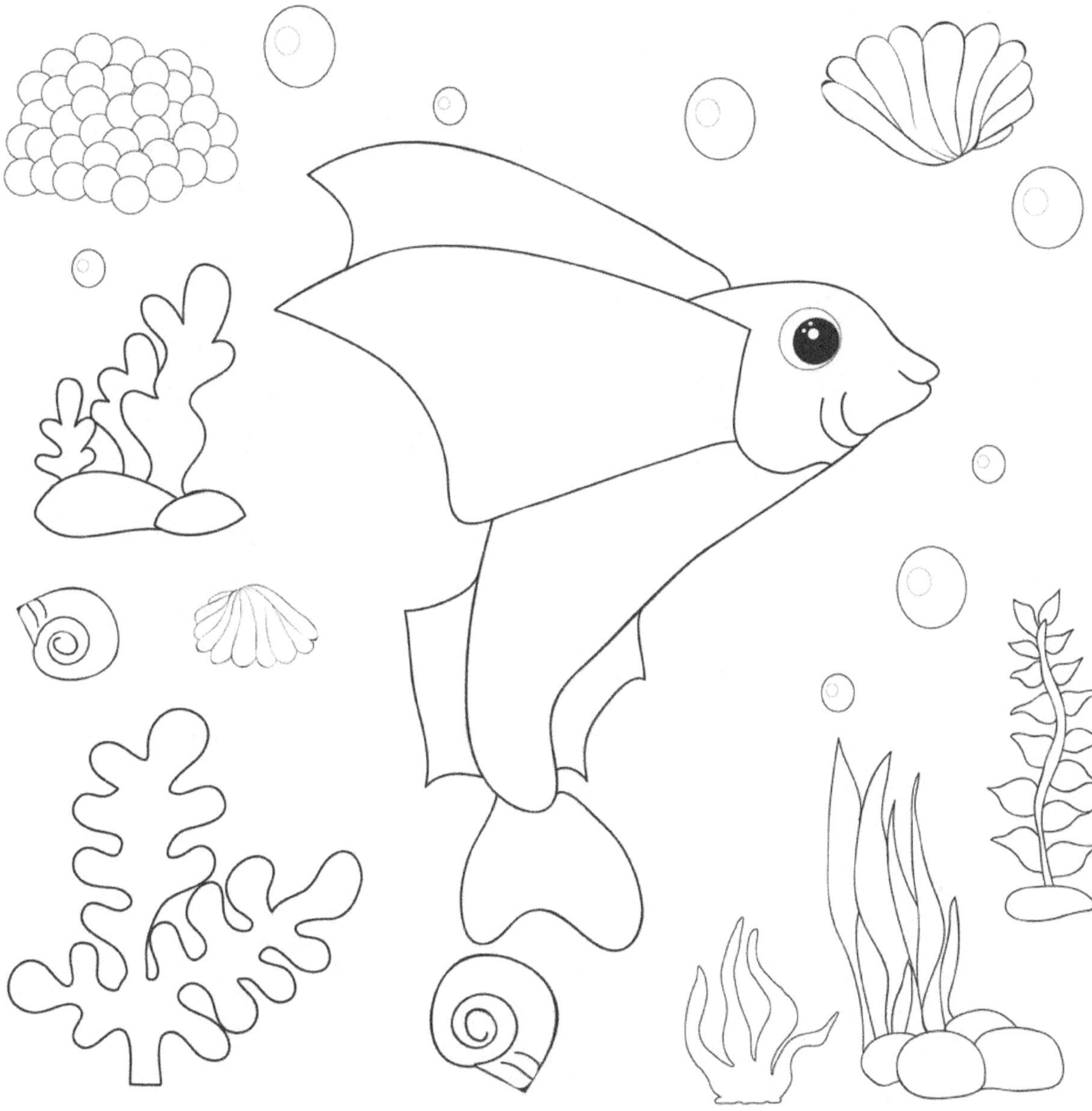

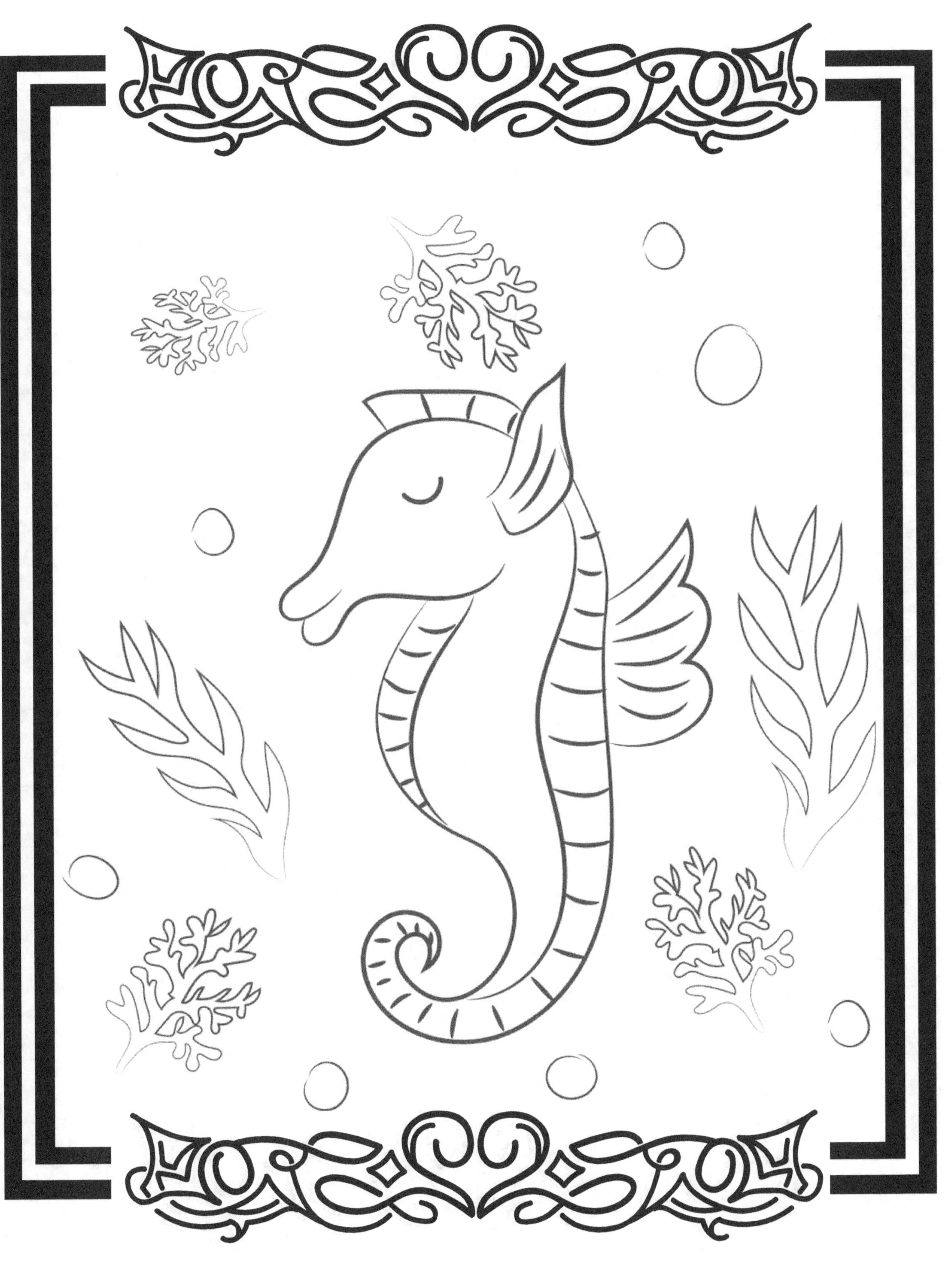

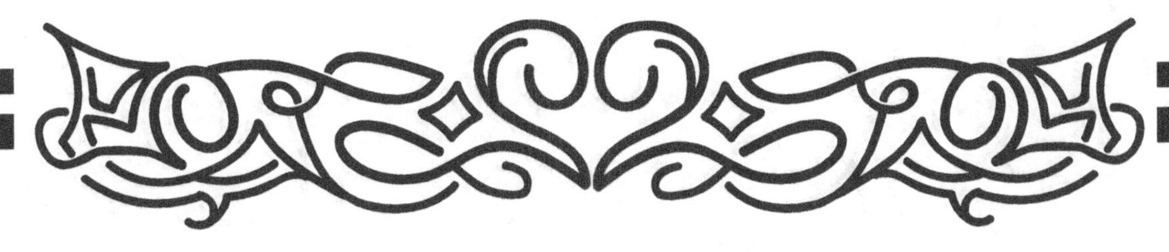

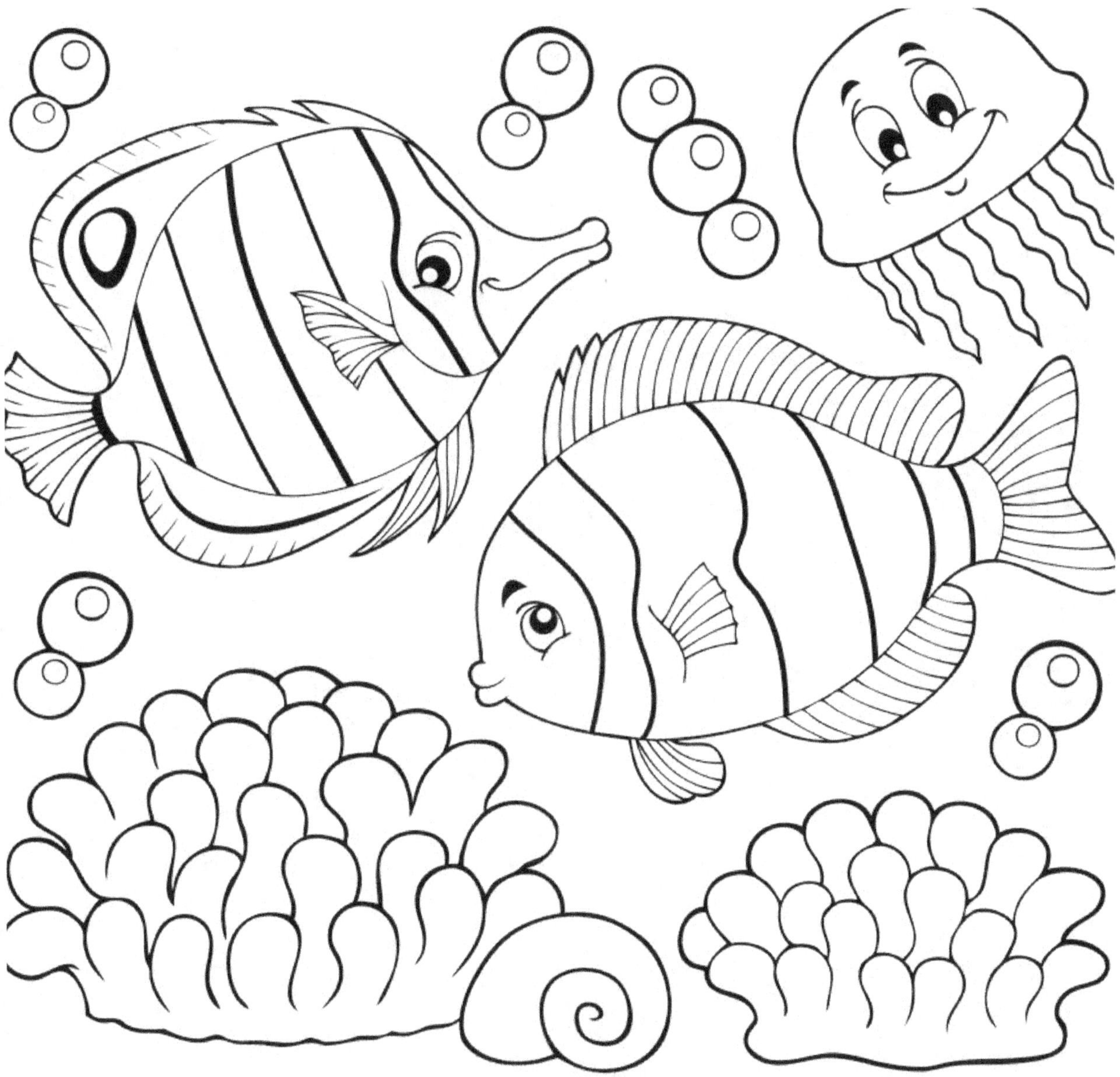

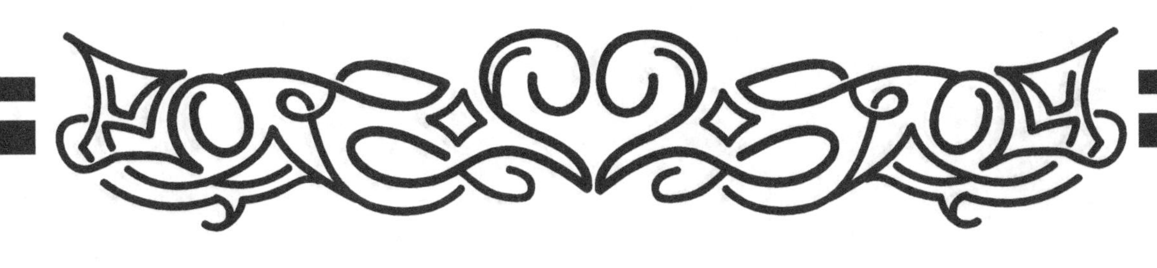

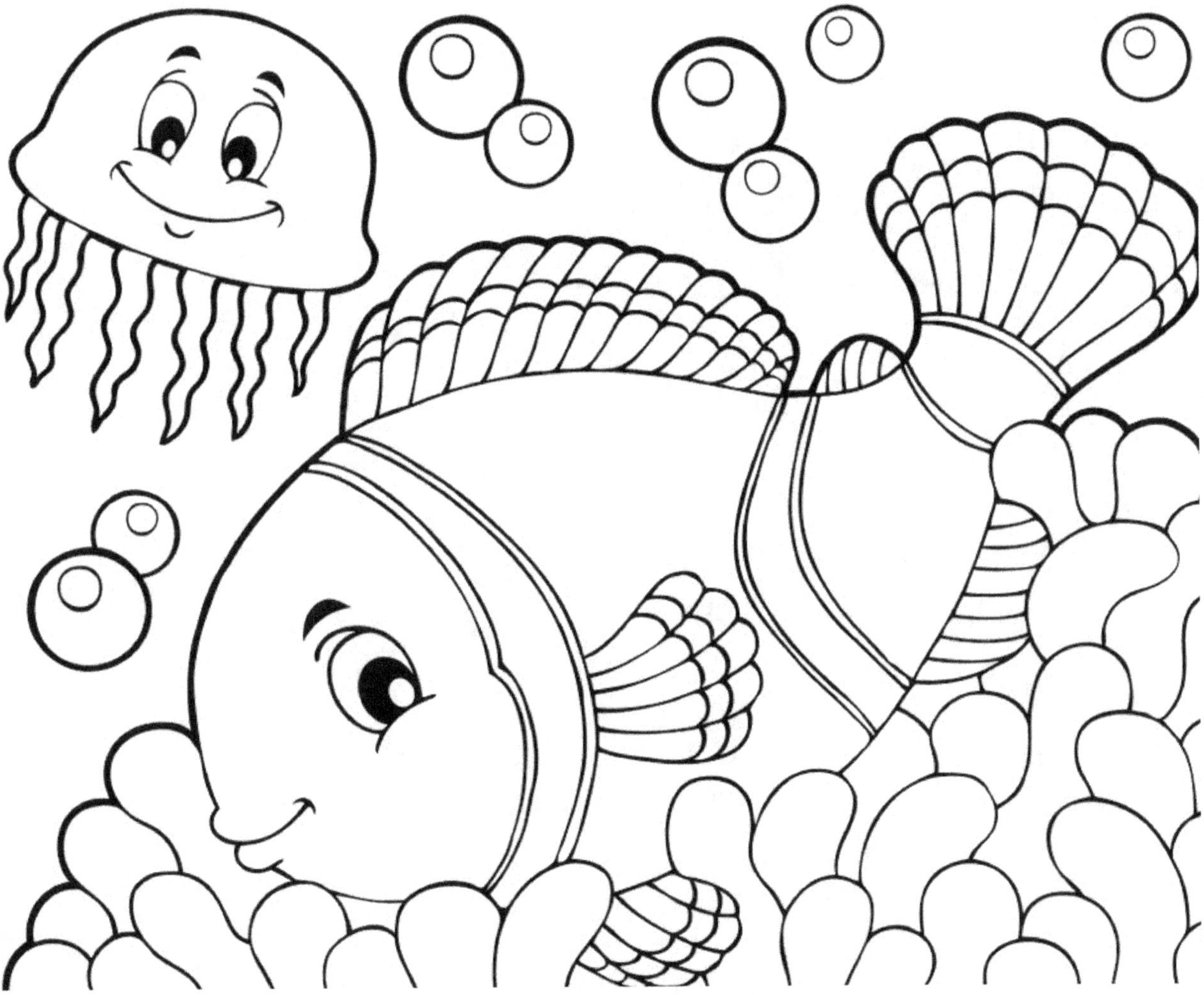

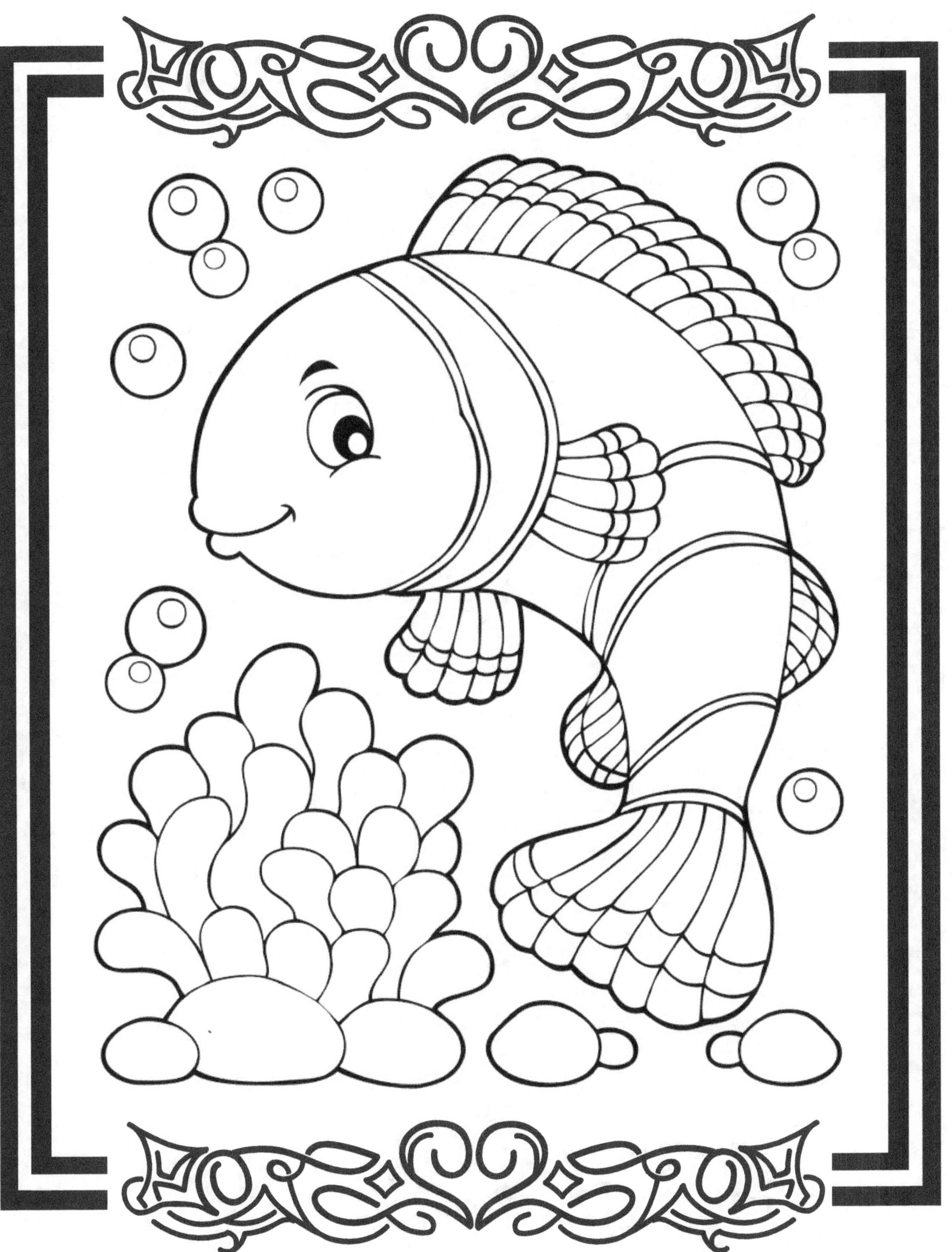

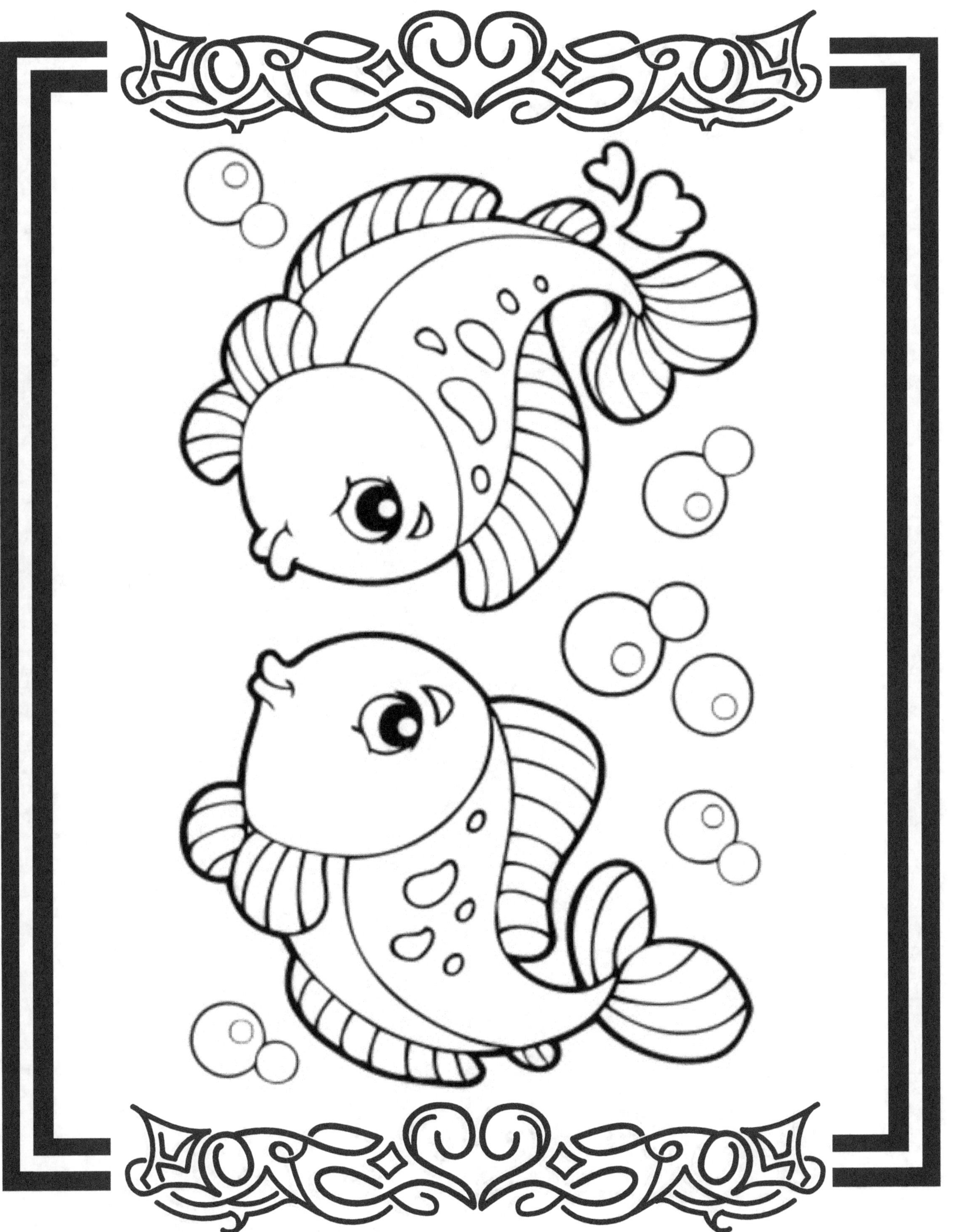

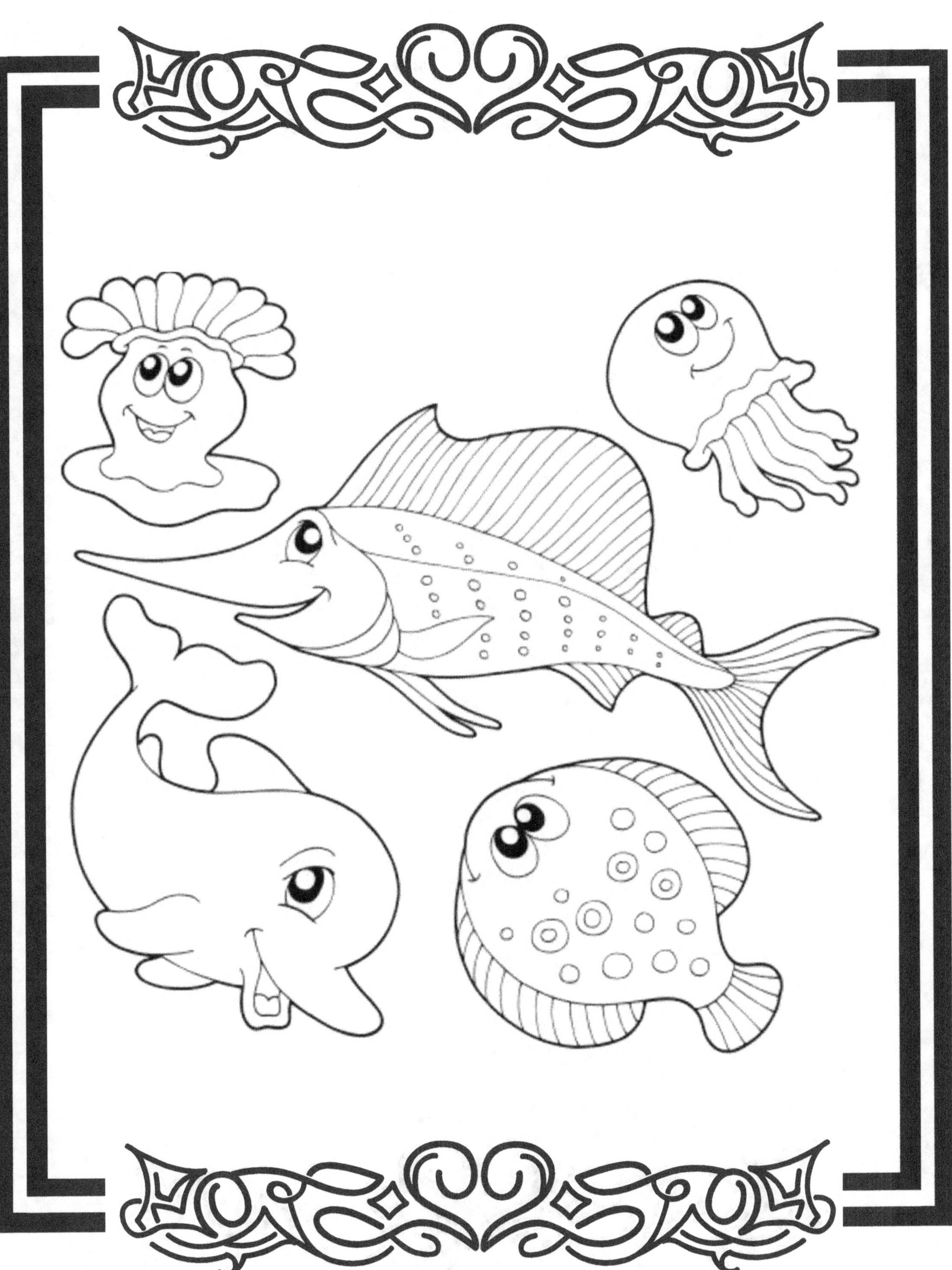

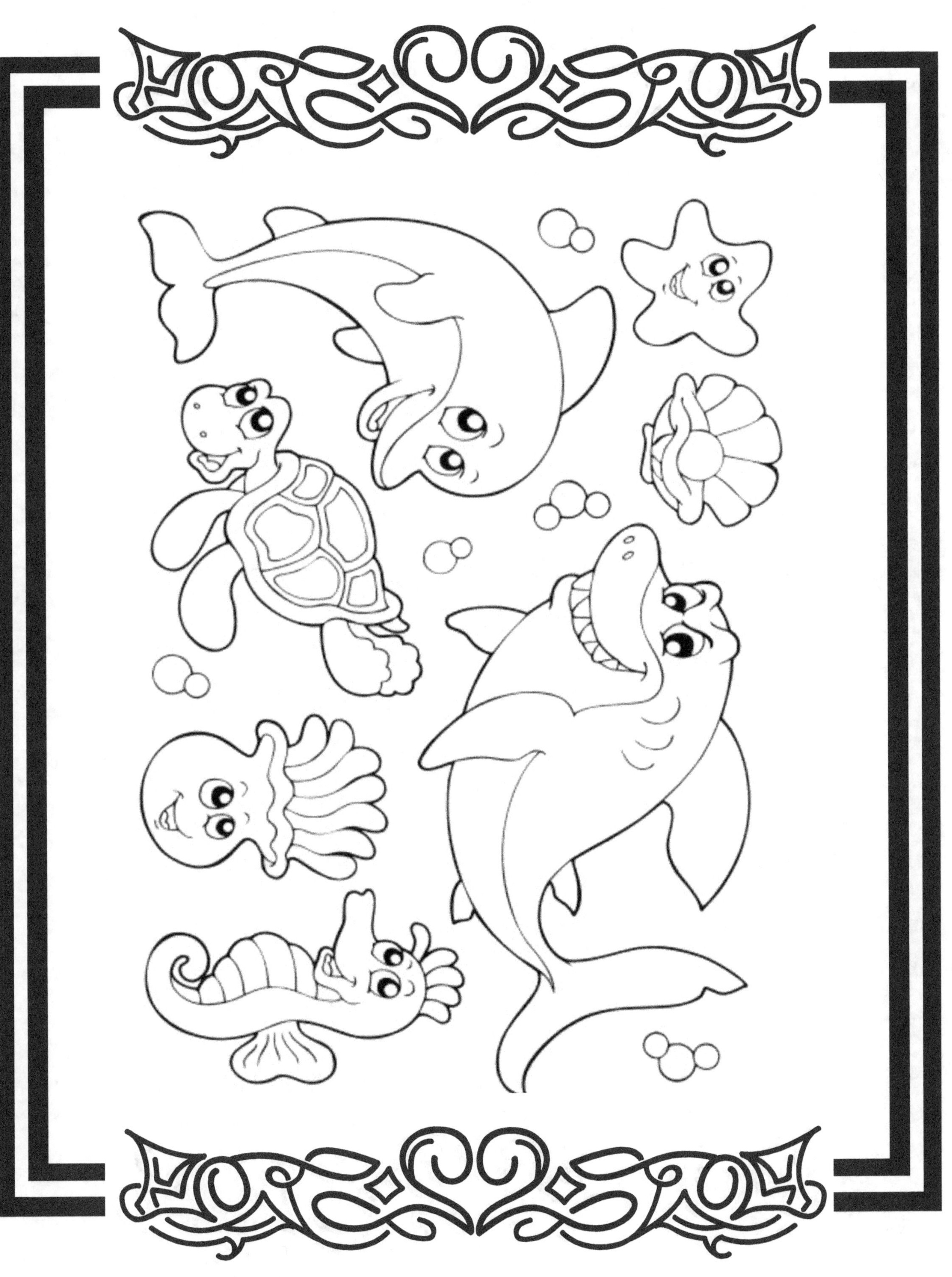

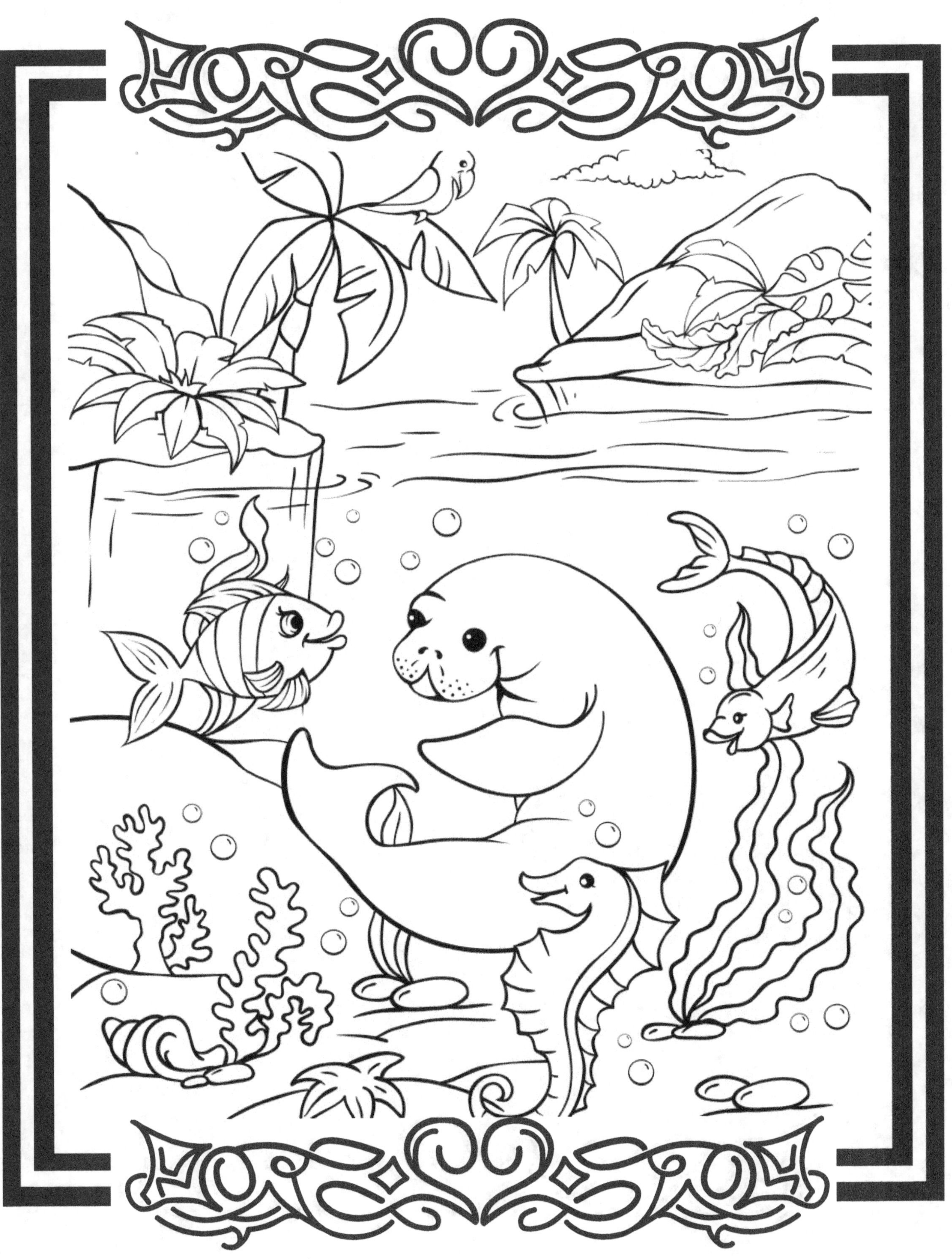

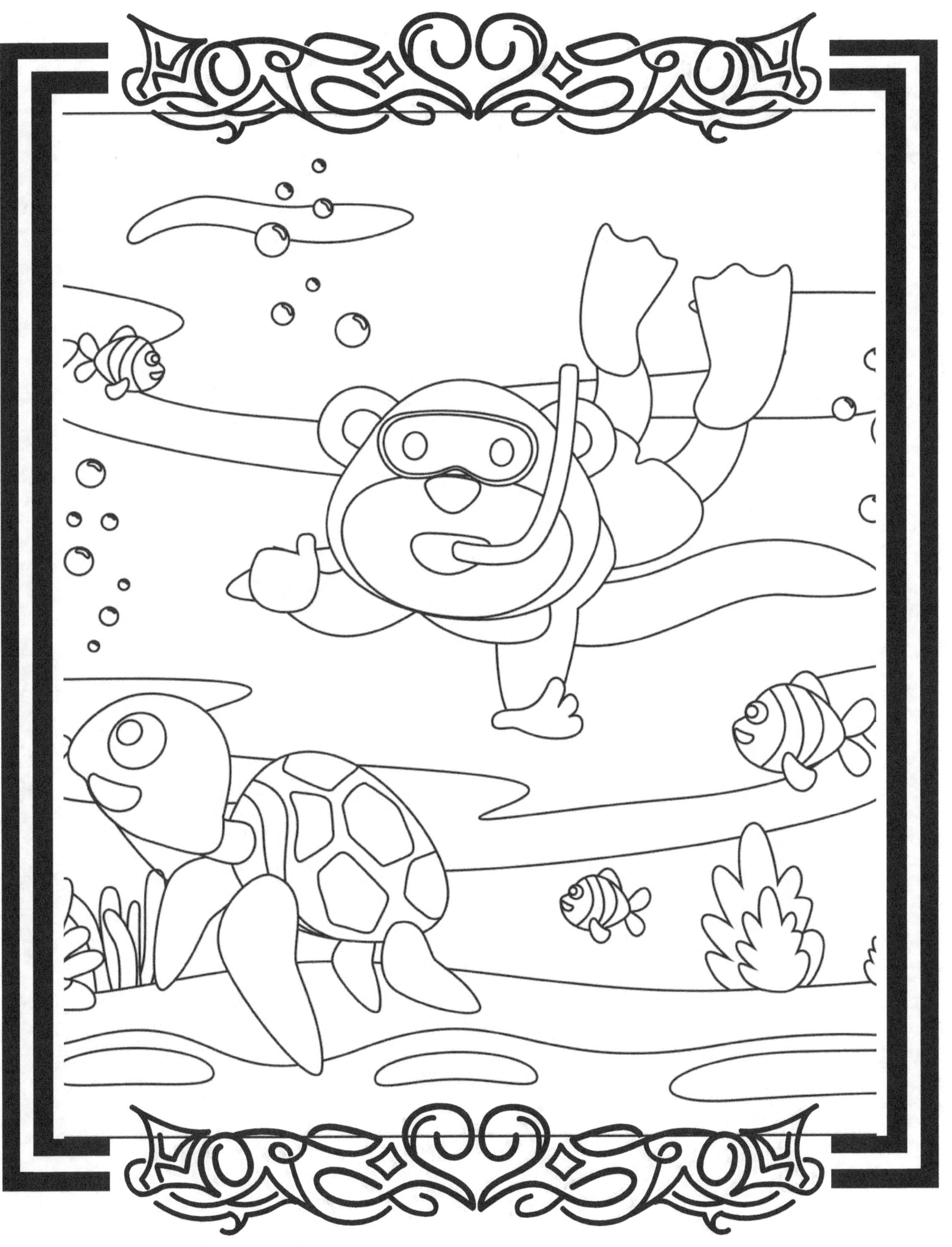

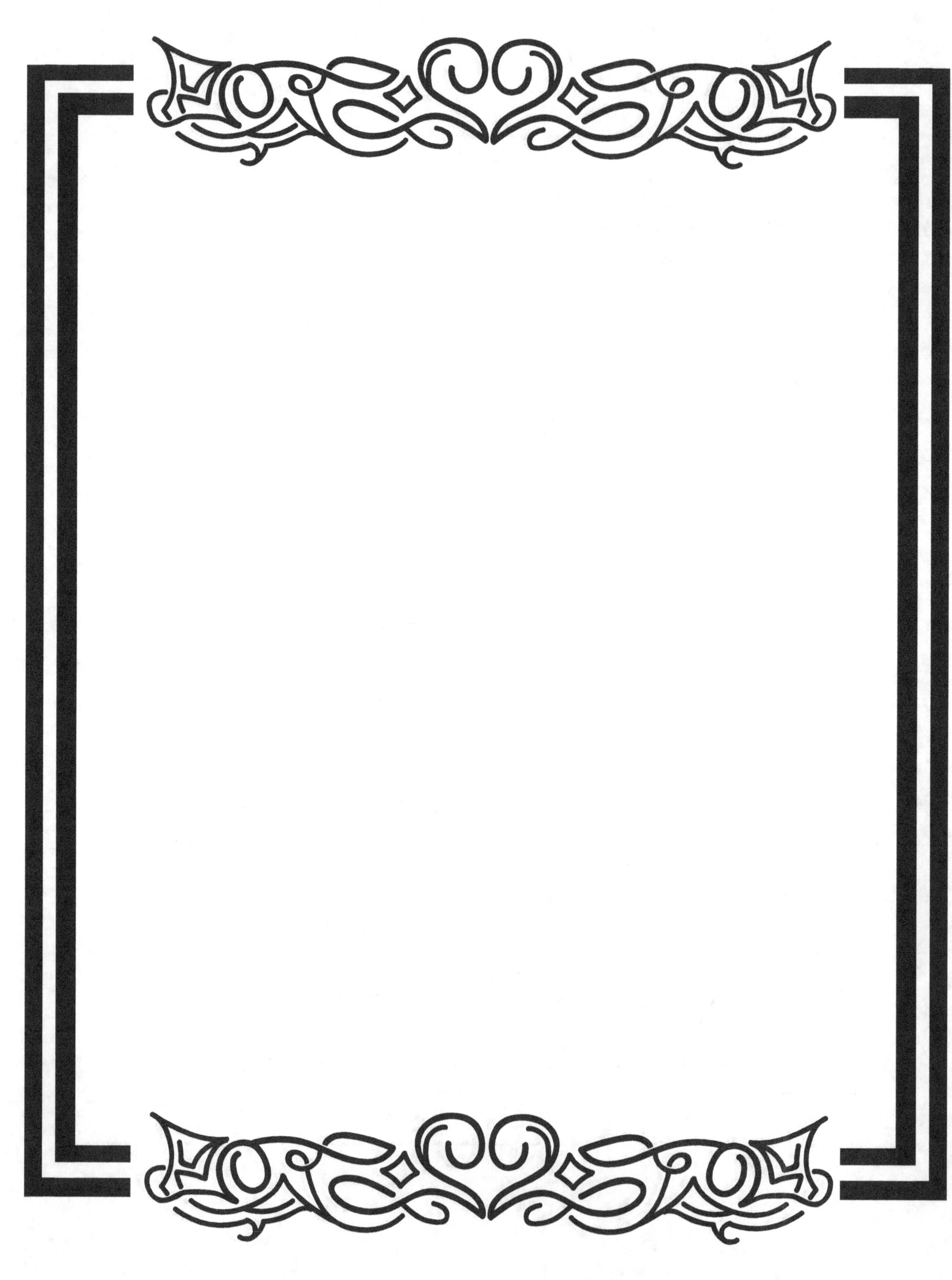

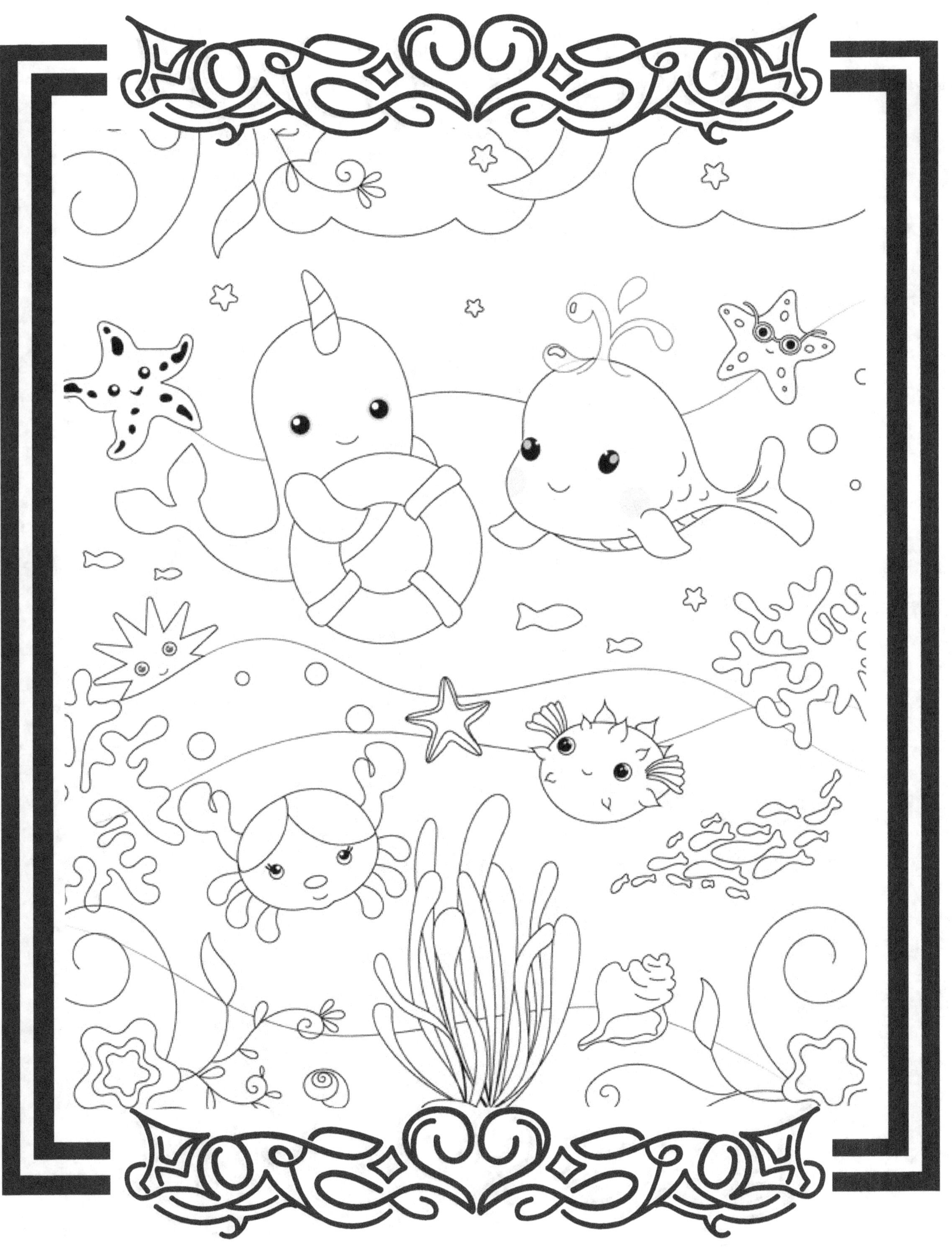

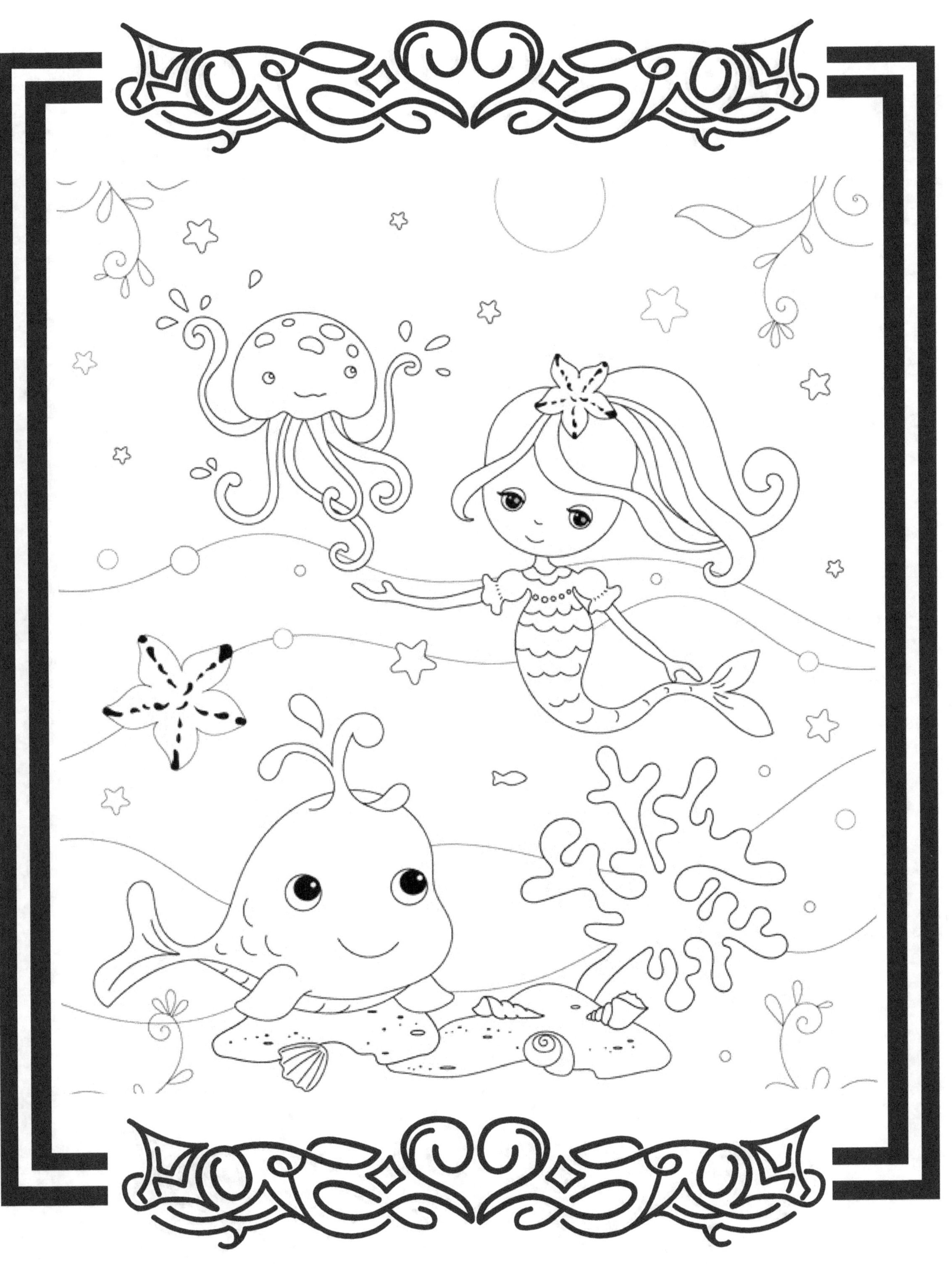

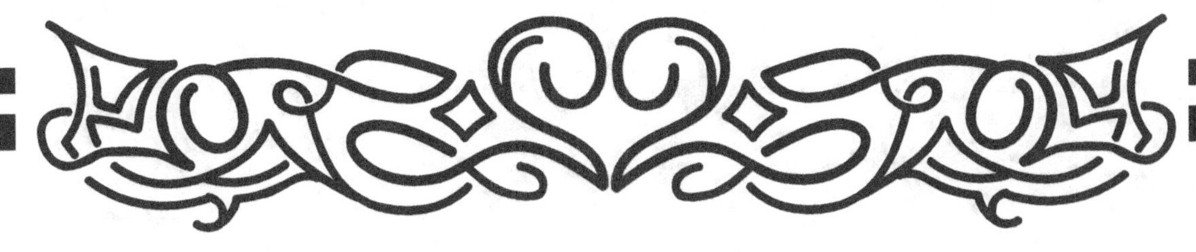

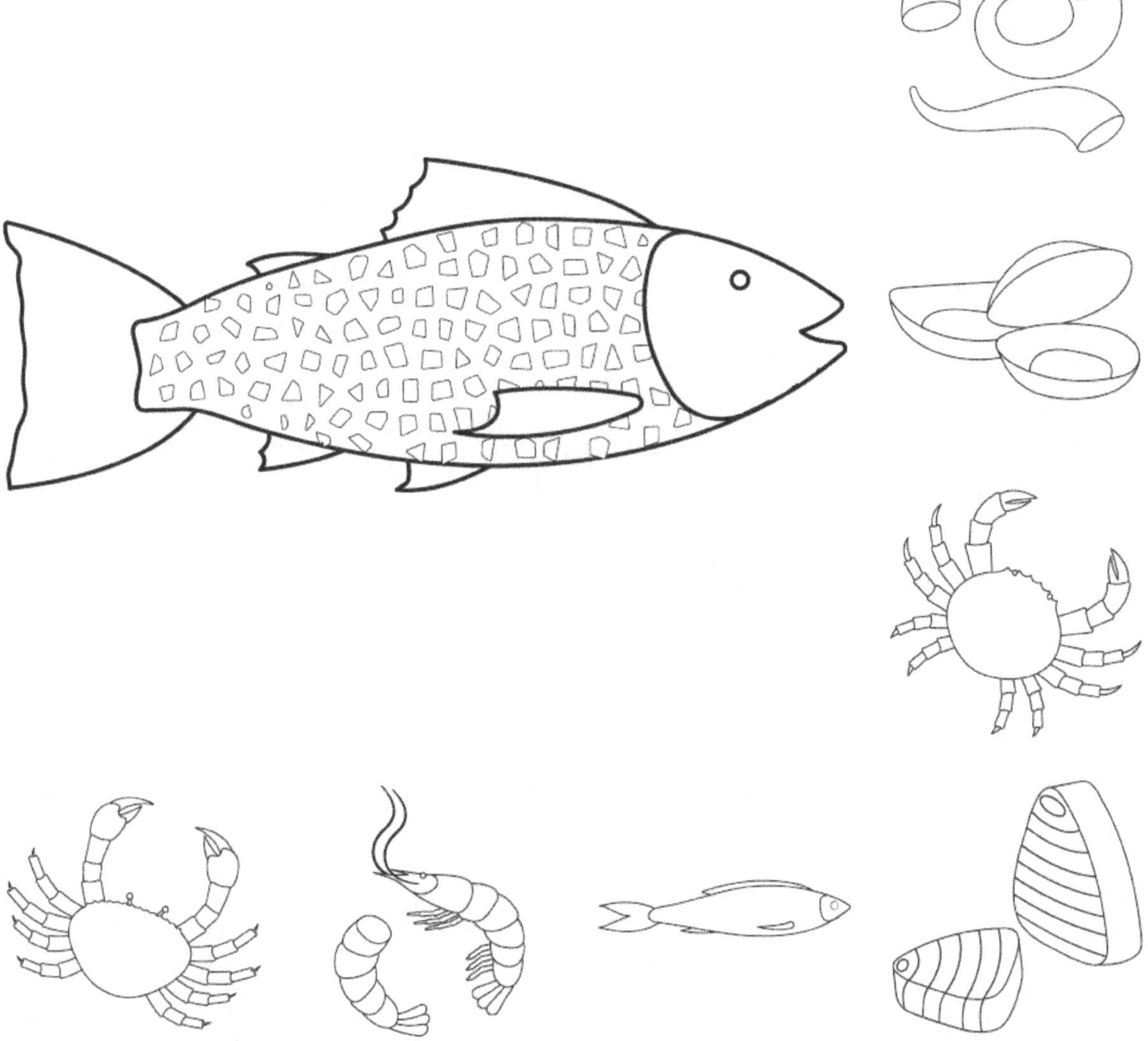

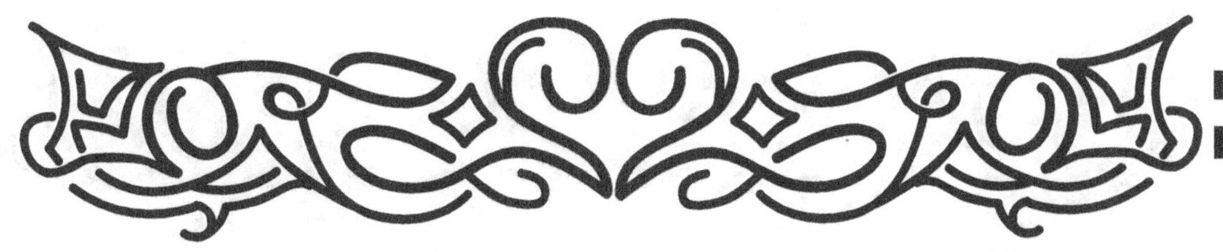

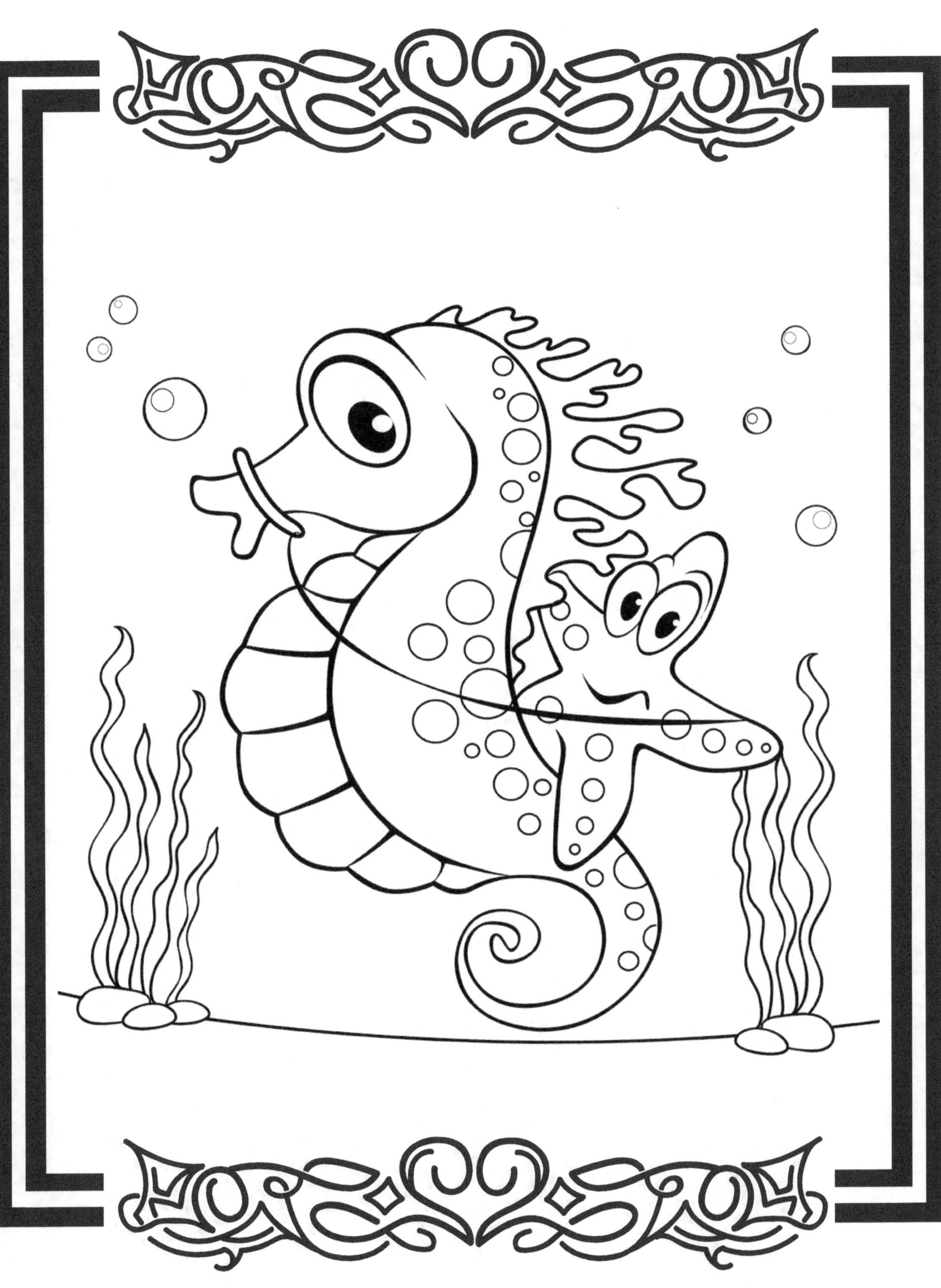

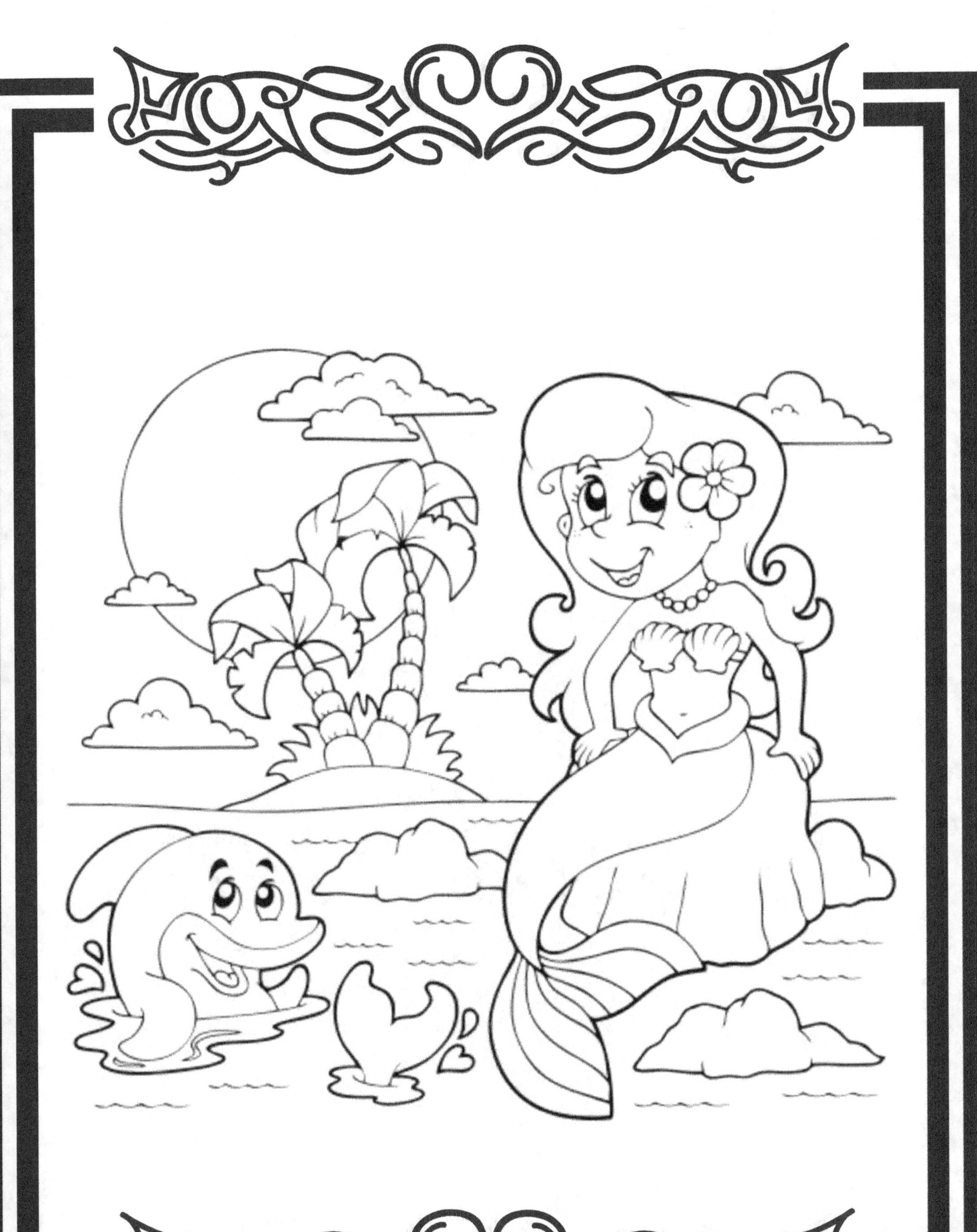

Thank You